Lifting the Veil

Mennonite Life in Russia Before the Revolution

Lifting the Veil

Mennonite Life in Russia
Before the Revolution

Mennonite Reflections

Mennonite Reflections

Mennonite Reflections is a monograph series dedicated to the preservation and publication of materials that explore the Mennonite experience. The series is published through the Institute of Anabaptist Mennonite Studies, Conrad Grebel College, University of Waterloo, in cooperation with Pandora Press.

The Silence Echoes: Memoirs of Trauma and Tears
 Edited and translated by Sarah Dyck, 1997.

Lifting the Veil: Mennonite Life in Russia Before the Revolution
 Jacob H. Janzen. Edited with an introduction by Leonard Friesen. Translated by Walter Klaassen,, 1998.

Lifting the Veil

Mennonite Life in Russia Before the Revolution

by

Jacob H. Janzen

Edited with an introduction by Leonard Friesen
Translated by Walter Klaassen

Published by Pandora Press,
Kitchener, Ontario
Co-published with Herald Press,
Scottdale, Pennsylvania/Waterloo, Ontario

Canadian Cataloguing in Publication Data

Janzen, Jacob H., 1878-1950
  Lifting the veil: Mennonite Life in Russia before the Revolution

(Mennonite Reflections, ISSN 1480-3895)
Translation of: Aus meinem Leben: Erinnerungen von J.H. Janzen
ISBN 0-9683462-1-9

1. Janzen, Jacob H., 1878-1950. 2. Mennonites – Russia – Biography.
I. Friesen, Leonard, 1956– . II. Klaassen, Walter, 1926– . III. Title.
IV. Series.

BX8143.J35A3 1998   289.7'092   C98-931441-3

LIFTING THE VEIL:
MENNONITE LIFE IN RUSSIA BEFORE THE REVOLUTION

Copyright © 1998 by Pandora Press
51 Pandora Avenue N.
Kitchener, Ontario, N2H 3C1
All rights reserved

Co-published with Herald Press,
Scottdale, Pennsylvania/Waterloo, Ontario

International Standard Book Number: 0-9683462-1-9
Printed in Canada on acid-free paper

Cover Photo: Jacob H. Janzen in his early twenties.

The pen and ink drawings used throughout are the work of Johannes Janzen,
elder brother of Jacob H. Janzen. They were used originally as chapter
heading illustrations in Jacob H. Janzen's book *Den Meine Augen haben
Deinen Heiland gesehen* (Hamburg: Christliches Verlagshaus Wiegand, n.d.).

Book and cover design by Clifford Snyder

05 04 03 02 01 00 99 98 10 9 8 7 6 5 4 3 2 1

Contents

Preface

I saw and met Jacob H. Janzen only once, in the summer of 1946, but really came under his influence nearly twenty years later when Ruth and I became members of the church of which he had been the founding bishop. There I met and came to appreciate and love members of his family. Although Jacob H. Janzen had long departed this life, I felt his presence each of the many times I preached from his pulpit over the years. It is, therefore, my great pleasure to help with the publication of these memoirs.

Aus meinem Leben: Erinnerungen von J.H. Janzen was first published in 1929 and printed in *Der Bote* in Rosthern, Saskatchewan. Numerous faded copies of this work are no doubt still extant, but nowadays can be read for the most part only by those who first bought them. I translated the book in 1992 in order to give new life to the memories of a giant who walked among us. If we see further today than he did, it is because we are standing on his shoulders.

Much of the work for this publication has been done by Professor Leonard Friesen of Wilfrid Laurier University. He regularized and modernized the transcription of the Russian adages and words; he provided most of the notes, the chapter titles which are not in the original and, most importantly, wrote the illuminating introduction which provides the setting for reading the memoirs. All of this had to be done to make these memoirs accessible to a new generation of readers.

Younger readers may find the introspective nature of some of the earlier sections unfamiliar and even uncomfortable. In writing this way,

Jacob H. Janzen was following old models of writing memoirs or diaries, a feature of which often was to recount one's struggle with sin and temptation. It was a kind of "confessional." In our time we are not accustomed to speaking about sin so openly and especially not about the "sins of childhood." If it strikes us as unhealthy or even as a sign of weakness it will be well for us to keep in mind that succeeding generations may feel just as uncomfortable with our silence on these matters. As the reader will see from the reading, for Jacob H. Janzen his "confessional" was neither unhealthy nor a sign of weakness.

Janzen was blessed with a very lively and active imagination and with a compulsion to write. He therefore had what Rainer Maria Rilke regarded as the most necessary qualification for a writer. This, combined with his excellent education, make these memoirs exciting reading. Janzen never parades his education, but here and there one can identify allusions to the thought of the great intellects of the past such as Michel de Montaigne and Immanuel Kant.

Readers may also be surprised at how passionately critical he was of the "Privilegium" and its results which he saw and experienced personally in the forestry service, the alternative open to Mennonites in lieu of military service. Like the writers of the Old Testament, he understood the revolutionary storm that overtook the Mennonites in Russia as God's judgement on their unfaithfulness. To this, too, we are unaccustomed in our day. That may be because we do not share to the same degree Jacob H. Janzen's conviction that God is the arbiter of history, and that those who sow the wind will reap the whirlwind.

This book was published with the financial support of members of the Janzen family. Two of Jacob H. Janzen's grandsons, James Neufeld and Philip Neufeld, made a special contribution to this project by the donation of their editorial and critical skills. Their valuable collaboration is gratefully acknowledged.

All of us who worked on bringing this memoir to you, Leonard Friesen, Arnold Snyder and Pandora Press and myself, hope it will contribute to better understanding of a piece of Mennonite history from the pen of a man who both passionately loved and sternly warned his people.

Walter Klaassen
Epiphany, 1998

Introduction

It was on a frosty autumn day in late October of 1901 that Jacob Janzen set out from the village of Pastwa for his parents' home in Gnadenfeld. He was accompanied by his wife, Helene, and they drove in silence past harvested fields lightly covered by a morning mist. Both craved the solitude of the morning. He later recalled that it was as if their horses understood their need for silence, and continued on without direction. The previous evening had witnessed a terrible event for this young couple, as their first child, Maria, had died of scarlet fever at less than two years of age. Grief surely accompanied them on that day. In his despair at the moment of Maria's death, Janzen had cried out: "O God, if You are, reveal Yourself to me and help me!" But would a response be forthcoming?

Miraculously, one was, and it was able to turn one of the darkest times in Janzen's life into a moment of deliverance and Christian conversion. In the midst of his mourning, he felt the quiet certainty that God had heard their cries. His once empty soul had mysteriously been filled by something too precious to be seen or touched. In a quiet way, he now surrendered himself to what he later described as "the blessedness of the Coming One." So fortified, Jacob was able to face this great tragedy, his pupils in the coming days, and any other obstacle that confronted him in the months and years ahead. He knew with utter certainty that he had entered "the enchanted zone of love."

Who was this man who experienced love at a time of sorrow? Where had he come from, and whither did he travel? What interest might any of this have for people living in another country, and in another time from the one described in this memoir?

The road that Jacob and Helene Janzen travelled that day connected two villages in the eastern portion of the Molotschna settlement in Imperial Russia. The settlement itself dated back to 1804, when over 200 Mennonite families emigrated from Prussia to this prairie region north of the Sea of Azov. What attracted them were the promises offered up by the Imperial Russian government of free land, freedom of religion, and a permanent exemption from military service. The land was highly conducive to settlement and held the promise of future prosperity. The soil was rich, covered with succulent grasses, and available in abundance. Markets and port cities were nearby, and eager to purchase the goods produced on Mennonite farms. Before long, nineteen villages had been established.

After difficult beginnings, the Molotschna Mennonites soon prospered, and in fact became model agriculturalists in the empire. More Mennonites continued to emigrate from Prussia to the Molotschna colony as its reputation grew, until the Russian state forbade further settlement in the 1840s.

It would be a mistake, however, to consider all of the Mennonites who settled in the Molotschna to have been similar in outlook. Those who arrived last from Prussia in the mid 1830s were, at the same time, those who had lived the longest under Prussian influence. In some cases, as with the Mennonite minister, Wilhelm Lange, they had converted from Lutheranism within years of their emigration. As a result, they were immediately seen as distinct from their co-religionists who had settled in the Molotschna two generations earlier. For one thing, the 1830s immigrants were more urbanized, and accustomed to a richer cultural life. For another, they brought distinctly Lutheran influences to the Molotschna, including a strong emphasis on personal piety and grace.

Not surprisingly, they settled in separate villages within Molotschna, and Gnadenfeld especially soon became a centre of religious innovation for the empire's Mennonites. Other villages in Gnadenfeld's orbit included Rudnerweide and Pastwa. Contemporaries described Gnadenfeld as a place of "progressive religious life." Some were drawn to it; others viewed it as an affront to long held religious sensitivities of hard work and humble modesty within the community. But in Gnadenfeld, at least, the progressive voices won the day. Thus, a minister from the Gnadenfeld congregation, Heinrich Dirks, became the first foreign Mennonite missionary when he was sent to south-east Asia in 1869. Others were regularly sent back to the German states for university education, and to reinforce the connection between Mennonites and the cultural world of their former homeland. This contact between Mennonites from Gnadenfeld and the cultural and religious world of Prussia was so strong that other Mennonites often referred to them as "Lutheran-Mennonites."

Nowhere was the connection between Mennonite and non-Mennonite worlds more apparent than in the formation of the "Brotherhood School," which was opened in 1857 in Gnadenfeld. This secondary school, which was quickly deemed to be one of the most progressive in the Mennonite world, had actually been inspired by revival meetings a decade earlier when Edward Wuest, himself a Lutheran, had visited the region. His fervent preaching reinforced those who stressed personal faith, the belief in Christ crucified, and the assurance of personal salvation. His followers among Mennonites, known as the "Wuest brethren," founded Gnadenfeld's "Brotherhood School."

Not surprisingly, it continued to advance notions of personal piety and individual progress. As a training centre for Mennonite elementary school teachers, it soon had a profound influence on the most progressive elements of Mennonite society. Put another way, it was a place where beliefs in individual initiative and free enterprise could be nurtured, whether in religious or economic matters, and all to the delight of some and consternation of others.

From modest beginnings, the teacher training programme in Gnadenfeld quickly influenced the direction of schools throughout the Molotschna colony. One such was located on the private estate of Steinbach, which was one of three private Mennonite estates located within the settlement. Steinbach had actually been awarded to Klaas Wiens, the first administrative head of the Molotschna colony, by Tsar Alexander I in 1818 as a reward for the economic leadership already shown by Mennonites. His nephew, Pieter Schmidt, inherited the estate and continued to stress "progressive" ideas. In 1838 he established a private school at Steinbach which was directly linked to the Gnadenfeld

"Lutheran-Mennonite" community. A key role in founding the school was played by Friedrich Lange, who had arrived in Gnadenfeld from Prussia in 1837, and been named minister of the Gnadenfeld Mennonite church the following year. For much of the Imperial period Steinbach school was considered part of the Gnadenfeld school society, and attracted pupils from the Russian nobility as well as from other Mennonite private estates.

By now the reader might be wondering what the relevance is of Molotschna, Gnadenfeld, Steinbach, "Lutheran-Mennonites" and progressivism to an introduction to a memoir written by Jacob Heinrich Janzen. The intent here, of course, is to provide the reader with a context for understanding Janzen's life and work. Yet even a brief overview places Janzen firmly within this world of pietistic "Lutheran-Mennonites." He was, to begin with, born on 18 March 1878 on the private estate of Steinbach, where his father, Heinrich J. Janzen, taught in the private school mentioned above.[1] In the first chapter of his autobiography, Janzen describes the love and devotion that he still had toward his parents. His father is described as physically infirm, but intellectually and spiritually vibrant: "The more his life sped to its end and the more frail he became physically, the more vigorously he spread about him an atmosphere of a vibrant, genuine, practical piety, full of the joy of life." By contrast, his mother is portrayed as "intimate," "understanding everything . . . the heart of the family." Both were exceptional people, and help us understand Jacob's later flowering.

Heinrich Janzen was born in 1844 in the Molotschna village of Ladekopp. His forebears had migrated to the Russian empire in 1804, when they had been among the earliest settlers in the Molotschna colony, though not initially from Gnadenfeld. Heinrich was unusually talented as an artist of sketches and oil paintings, and a writer of devotional materials, hymns, and poems. He was also physically incapacitated for much of his life, having barely escaped death in a childhood accident when he was crushed by rollers in his father's mill.

---

[1] There is some confusion regarding the date of Jacob's birth, sometimes listed as March 19, 1878. Jacob was born March 6, 1878 according to the "Old Style" or Julian calendar. When Russia converted to the Gregorian calendar in 1918, all birthdays up to February 28, 1900 (O.S.) were to be converted by adding twelve days; thirteen days were to be added to birthdays thereafter. In Jacob's case, thirteen days were added where the correct number should have been twelve. His correct birth date by the Gregorian calendar is March 18.

In 1865 Heinrich Janzen married Maria Dirks, the sister of the Gnadenfeld minister and foreign missionary, Heinrich Dirks. Thereafter, he maintained a lifelong connection with the Gnadenfeld church, even though he was occasionally absent for long periods. It was while Heinrich was teaching at Steinbach that Jacob was born. In 1880, however, Heinrich moved back to Gnadenfeld where he was ordained as minister. In that same year, Heinrich began a teaching assignment at the Gnadenfeld *Zentralschule*, which continued until 1884.

Regardless of the road that followed from here, it was clear that Jacob Janzen was born to parents who were unusual by the standards of the larger Mennonite world. He was surrounded at the outset by "Lutheran-Mennonites" who valued high culture, the literary arts, and believed in faithfulness and the assurance of individual salvation. One can already anticipate a world in which Jacob felt profoundly connected to the larger Mennonite community even while serving as a gentle and at times distant, critic of it.

In 1884 Heinrich and Maria Janzen relocated their family to the Vladimirov *Forstei* (forestry camp), where Heinrich served as chaplain for seven years. It is important to account for these camps, given the role that they play in Jacob Janzen's early life, and the attention that he devotes to them in this memoir. These camps represented a negotiated solution to a difficult problem in relations between Mennonites and the Russian state, which had begun a vigorous period of reform following its defeat in the Crimean war in 1856. This reform period culminated in the military reform in 1874, by which St. Petersburg opted for the creation of a small standing army with a very large reserve force. At the same time, the state sought to simplify the empire's complicated social structure by reducing the host of categories into which the population had been divided previously – including state peasant, crown peasant, colonist, military settler, and so on – in favour of the single designation of peasant.

Mennonites knew immediately that the loss of special designations spelled the end of their "permanent" guarantee of military exemption. In response, a third of the empire's Mennonites emigrated to North America in 1874. Those who stayed negotiated with the government, which had become alarmed by the emigration fever gripping the colonies. After months of intense discussions, St. Petersburg finally conceded the right of Mennonites to maintain their military exemption. In exchange, those Mennonites drafted were required to report to mobile forestry camps, known as *Forstei*, that were established throughout New Russia, as the region was called. Forestry camps were deemed especially important given the barren nature of much of New Russia. In previous decades, Mennonite economies had flourished, in part because of the active forestation projects that had been initiated on their own estates and villages. St. Petersburg now hoped that Mennonites would provide this service for all of New Russia.

For their part, Mennonites were reassured by the ability to avoid military service of any kind, even if those in the forestry service were required to wear uniforms and sleep in barracks. Mennonites hoped that the segregation of Mennonites would assist in the preservation of their distinct religious values and identity, especially as each camp was to have an *Ökonom-Prediger*[2] assigned to it for the spiritual and material supervision of the Mennonite youth. Beyond this formal title, the young men in the camps most commonly referred to these overseers as *Papa* (Daddy). In addition, Mennonites were expected to pay for the construction and maintenance of the barracks, and provide food and clothing for Mennonites stationed there.

After long and often difficult negotiations, the first Mennonites were officially placed in the forestry programme in 1881. By that time, there were two camps in New Russia and a third, Vladimirov, was opened in February of 1882. This latter camp, situated on the west side of the Dnieper river, was about 150 kilometres from the Molotschna colony, and served as Jacob Janzen's home from the time that he was four years old until the age of thirteen. Later, as an adult (Chapter 5), Jacob was sent to the Alt-Berdjaner *Forstei*, located much closer to his home, on the south-west corner of the Molotschna colony.

Despite the high goals set for these camps, Jacob Janzen consistently described them as places without any meaningful function where Mennonite youths often behaved in the most deplorable manner. He concluded that the camps were morally illegitimate, and had a deteriorating influence on precisely those young people they were designed to protect. In fact, many contemporaries were discouraged by the low morale that was widespread throughout these camps. Some muttered complaints about living conditions, while others bemoaned the

---

[2] The title literally meant "economist-preacher." The *Ökonom-Prediger* was both camp administrator and chaplain.

access that the youth had to alcohol. Within months of its opening, the Vladimirov camp was identified as being in desperate need of spiritual direction, and likely precipitated the call for as important a figure as Jacob's father, Heinrich.

At the age of seven, Jacob was sent from the Vladimirov *Forstei* to a Mennonite village school, and was able to return to his parents only on occasional weekends. He describes his years of late childhood and adolescence variously as akin to being in a "cold far country" or "between the dark shadow of sin and the bright beams of love." Although on the edge of despair at times, he was always brought back by the love of those around him, most especially his parents. In a particularly poignant section at the end of Chapter 2, Janzen recalled the tragic fate that befell so many of his school mates from this time.

Jacob Janzen finished his elementary school education determined to be a naval engineer. His grades certainly warranted such a goal. Unfortunately, a major obstacle presented itself in the form of his father's steady physical deterioration, which had compelled Heinrich and Maria to relocate from the Vladimirov *Forstei* to their home village of Gnadenfeld in 1891. Thereafter, his parents were sustained by a modest income derived from the little house and yard that they possessed within the village, and a small painting business that Heinrich managed. Desperate to find financial support for his son to pursue his dream of engineering, Heinrich sought out patrons from within the community. It was a pivotal moment in Jacob's life.

Suddenly aware of the great strain his ambitious goals had placed on his parents, and too proud to accept a patron's support, Jacob announced to his parents that he was quite content to become a teacher. He described this decision as "his first great sacrifice," the end of childhood. In September of 1894 Jacob travelled to the regional centre of Melitopol, where he passed the teacher examinations at the tender age of sixteen, and was assigned to the village school in Rudnerweide. After three years, he was reassigned to the neighbouring village of Pastwa, where he taught until 1903.

Jacob later recalled that this transition from childhood to adulthood – marked by his time in Rudnerweide and Pastwa – was very difficult for him. There was much that he valued of this time, including the ongoing support of friends and family, and the intellectual engagement with his pupils. Above all, he cherished big questions: a pupil once asked in Bible class why God allowed Cain to murder Abel. It touched a chord with Janzen, who saw in this question a reflection of his own puzzlement about human motive. Why did people not always do the right thing? The question was especially timely because of the confusion in Janzen's own life. His teaching position seemed to him more like a career failure than a triumph, and therefore his heart was often not in it. He had developed an understanding of the Christian faith in which he had been raised, but not in a way that had made a difference in his own life. He found temptation's call hard to resist.

Adding to his confusion was the turmoil found within the Russian empire. The late nineteenth century was a time of remarkable change in the empire, in which a new world was being superimposed upon an old one. The reforms mentioned above were an important part of this process. So also were the rapid pace of industrialization unleashed in the late nineteenth century, and the slow but steady progress observed in peasant agriculture. Some within the larger society were optimistic about the future of Russian society; others – and nihilists among them – believed that all noble ideals and religious beliefs were folly and in need of destruction. The location of Rudnerweide and Pastwa on the eastern edge of the Molotschna Mennonite settlement no doubt eased his contact with revolutionary elements beyond the village. Yet all the while his conscience continued to steer him away from "the paths of darkness," until he rejected it totally.

Even so, he had not found his way into "the bright beams of love." That awaited two events: his marriage to Helene Braun in 1899, and the death of their eldest child, Maria, which began this introduction. Readers will find the account of his conversion (Chapter 3) to be heartfelt and personal, though the words he uses to describe it come directly from the larger pietistic world of his upbringing. He now no longer found himself torn between "sin and love," but totally within "the enchanted zone of love." As befitted a new life, Jacob and Helene departed from Pastwa in 1903 for a new assignment at the village school in Friedensdorf, where he stayed until 1905. It also was in the shadow and under the pleasant progressive influence of Gnadenfeld, less than twelve kilometres away.

In 1906, at the age of twenty-eight, Jacob was ordained to the ministry of the Gnadenfeld church, and two years later began to teach at the School for Girls at Ohrloff-Tiege. Opened in 1822, the secondary school at Ohrloff-Tiege, in the western part of the Molotschna, had long been a centre for progressive ideas among Mennonites. It now provided him with employment until war and revolution pulled him away from the Molotschna. Jacob's fervent conversion provided a solid foundation for his role in the church and school, but it did not result in a tension-free life. Janzen's commitment to the introduction of more progressive ideas resulted in a number of innovations, especially Bible studies and evening hymn sings. Both are discussed at length in the text (Chapter 4).

To understand how these seemingly harmless phenomena threatened traditional Mennonite society, one has to understand that for centuries almost all religious leaders had avoided the introduction of new forms into church life. Instead, it was argued that the faith and practice of past generations were adequate for contemporary believers as well. This had caused a very real dilemma for many of the more "progressive" Mennonites, especially those in the circle of villages in and around Gnadenfeld.

In 1860 a portion of those Mennonites denounced the established church leaders and argued that the reliance on past traditions had resulted in the corruption of the entire body. Under such circumstances, the Mennonite Brethren church was born, and quickly introduced innovations such as four-part choral singing and evening Bible studies. In fact, choral singing emerged naturally within Gnadenfeld, as choirs were mentioned in the earliest records of settlement, although they disappeared soon thereafter until late in the century.

Those that remained in the "traditional" Mennonite church, and still committed to innovate where possible, faced a significant problem: how might changes be introduced in a church committed to conservatism, and suspicious of change? In Chapter 4, Janzen relates the manner in which he introduced Bible studies and choral singing. Beyond these, Jacob also made an important contribution through his literary efforts, by which he followed in his father's footsteps.

Ironically, fiction appealed to Janzen as a means by which he could, in his own words, "lift the veil, to look into the causes, to study character, to grasp something I've seen and share it with others." Janzen saw all Mennonites around him in the same struggle between good and evil, and lamented the many occasions when they, individually and corporately, were unfaithful to God's calling. Much of this was revealed in his literary activity, which began with a one-act drama written for the Ohrloff-Tiege girls school in 1912. As one might expect, Mennonites were not always receptive to such criticisms, or to the literary evenings where they were voiced. For a time he was even removed from his ministerial duties in the Gnadenfeld Church. Undaunted, Janzen simply took the ministerial leadership at Melitopol until he was reinstated.

In 1913 Jacob Janzen had the opportunity of a lifetime. He was able to travel to Germany to study an impressive range of subjects, including Lutheran theology, philosophy, and psychology, at the Universities of Greifswald and Jena. He was thirty-five at the time. It was an invigorating experience, even as it raised new questions about his ability to balance the Mennonite and Lutheran worlds that he had come to inhabit. He returned home to his family, which had stayed behind in the large teacher's quarters of the School for Girls in Ohrloff-Tiege. His family by then consisted of Heinrich (b. 1903), Erna (b. 1905), Helga (b. 1907), Elisabeth (b. 1909), Alexandra (b. 1911), and Sieghard (b. 1912). Two others, including Maria, had died in infancy. Family members long remembered this period in glowing terms, and the future seemed bright. Another child, Martha, was born in November of 1917, but by then Jacob Janzen's world had been turned upside down.

World War I, which began in the fall of 1914, had a devastating impact on the Russian empire, as the excitement caused by initial victories was soon stifled by a string of defeats that resulted in huge losses. One year later Jacob Janzen was drafted into the Russian army, and was compelled to serve within the *Forstei* (Chapter 5). It served as a return, of sorts, to his childhood, except that Vladimirov was exchanged for the Alt-Berdjaner *Forstei,* not far from the Molotschna village of Altonau. Time had not mellowed Jacob's view of the *Forstei,* despite his father's previous endorsement of them. Much of this chapter deals with Janzen's claim that privileges embodied in the famous *Privilegium* – such as the exemption from military service – actually harmed Mennonite interests in the long run as they alienated Mennonites from their Russian and Ukrainian compatriots.

Was he correct in his judgement? Certainly there is a long tradition that found the root cause of terrible events in the sins or failings of the wounded party; hence Mennonites were responsible for the terrible fate that befell them. One need look no further than the thirteenth century Orthodox lament that the devastating Mongol invasion of the previous century had happened because of the sins of the Russian people. Yet, in the meantime historians have found other explanations to be more persuasive.

Similarly, in 1929 when Janzen penned this memoir, it appeared that the Imperial collapse and Bolshevik victory had been the logical and inevitable outcome of all previous Russian history. Under those circumstances, it is not surprising that Janzen, and many others, felt a sense of guilt for the collapse of the Russian empire. Mennonites were partially responsible for their own demise especially, in his view, as they lived in isolated islands on the great Russian steppe. For him, the *Forstei* were but symptoms of a larger illness.

Recent scholarship has done much to dispel this notion. There is now sound reason to see the impact of Mennonites in the region's development as largely positive, and the Bolshevik revolution as more of a fluke than an inevitable consequence of history. Peasants who were fortunate enough to have Mennonites as their neighbours, whether near the Khortitsa or the Molotschna colonies, were better off than than those peasants who lived farther away. Had Janzen been writing in our time, after the collapse of the Soviet Union, and with access to materials now available, his reflections might well have taken him in another direction.

What is clear is that the Russian state turned on Mennonites with the onset of World War I, as they were lumped together with all Germans; hence the harsh expropriation laws referred to in Chapter 5. It is also certain that many Mennonites ended up in the *Forstei* with virtually no commitment to pacifism. Others held Mennonite or Christian beliefs but were hardly prepared to put them into practice. Above all, Janzen bemoaned the occasions when Mennonites failed to live by the strict moral code he had established for himself.

Russia's war effort worsened as 1915 gave way to a new year, and suspicion of all those with a Dutch-Germanic background increased. After a brief visit to his home, Jacob was dispatched to Kursk, far in the northern reaches of the empire, where he remained until the end of the period described in this memoir. Conditions in the north were much more difficult than those which he had enjoyed in the warm south. Added turmoil was caused by the great physical gulf that now separated Janzen from his young family. It was also in the north that he became aware of his special skill as a "druggist" – a healer with natural remedies. He combined this role along with those of sometime cook, chaplain, purchaser, and accountant until the collapse of the Tsarist government in March of 1917.

Jacob returned home three months later, to a world in utter disarray. By the summer of 1917 centralized control had vanished in the empire. Though Janzen alludes to more recent events, including the death of his wife Helene in 1922, these are hardly described with the depth of reflection found elsewhere in this memoir. Nor does Janzen deal with his role as chaplain in the White Army during the Civil War period from July, 1919 until July, 1920, nor anything else prior to his emigration to Waterloo, Ontario, in November of 1924. Instead, he refers to it only as "a time of testing" (Chapter 7), whose only value was that it drew Mennonites closer to Christ.

Readers may wonder why the memoir ends where it does, and as abruptly as it does. It may be because the events of this relatively recent "time of persecution" were still too raw, too recent, for him to have come to terms with in 1929. Or perhaps Janzen had been drawn to reflections about life in his former homeland at the very time that Mennonites were establishing a new life in a new country. Finally, it is also possible that Janzen stopped abruptly because, as in a good sermon, he was less concerned with narrative and chronology than with meaning and significance. He himself wrote that he had wanted, in the pages of this memoir, to recall all that he had seen, and share it with others. As a recent immigrant to a new country, he felt the need to take his bearings, to reset his compass.

Having entered the sixth decade of his life, Janzen realized that nothing was more desirable than the assurance of God's leading. Nor was anything more worth striving for than the Kingdom of God, regardless of the obstacles that occasionally obstructed the way. It was a message that Jacob Heinrich Janzen first grasped while travelling from Pastwa to Gnadenfeld on a misty morning in October of 1901; and it was one that he carried with him to his death in Waterloo, Ontario, in February of 1950.

Leonard Friesen
Department of History
Wilfrid Laurier University

Chapter 1

Beginnings

[3] I sit in Prince Albert as a witness in a law case.[1] It has been going on for some years and appears as though it will never end.

I am firmly convinced that it will not come to an end in this session either, since the participants have not yet achieved what they intend.

But that is already a judgment, and I am not here to judge but only to be a witness in an apparently very trivial matter which has now, in the hands of the participants, grown to a major case. That's life.

I am in this through the fault of my own tongue, that restless evil full of deadly poison, which I have still not learned to keep sufficiently in

---

[1] The original text begins with this sentence, on page 3, following the title page and one blank page. The numbers within square brackets identify the page numbers of the original German text. The lawsuit Janzen refers to here was that between Friesen and Braun which lasted from 1925 to 1929. He was evidently called as a witness on behalf of Braun and as a supporter of David Toews. [See Frank H. Epp, *Mennonites in Canada, 1920-1940* (Toronto: Macmillan, 1982), 311-13]. At this time Janzen was bishop of the Waterloo-Kitchener United Mennonite Church in Waterloo, Ontario, and a prominent leader of Mennonites in Canada.

check. In a careless moment I had earlier admitted to having received a certain letter, and had not given it a second thought. It was only a few words I spoke, but I should not have spoken them. Because of those few words I have now had to travel thousands of miles. This brief thought, expressed in that simple, short sentence has now brought in its train a flood of twisted consequences, suspicions, false and accurate conclusions. It may even be that it was the occasion of criminal action. Having been inserted into a man's thinking, it may have stimulated other thoughts which were translated into plans from which came certain decisions which were then carried out. It may be that the crime came to be that way.

And even if not, my failure is a fact and cannot be changed. I can have only one judgment on my carelessness, whether the crime actually happened that way or only could have: I should have held my tongue at the right time. May God forgive me that I did not.

I now have a lot of time to reflect since my part in the court proceedings takes very little time. I have the rest of the time for myself since I take no pleasure in listening to the case. I am repelled by this trampling of the human soul. I suppose it has to be done, but if it is the obligation and [4] duty of some to do it, I believe I have the moral right to withdraw from it. I have enough of my own to do and do not need to take all of this upon me as well especially since, in the last analysis, it does not concern me.

And yet, I cannot avoid thinking about the case. I am not interested so much in the factual details, but chiefly in the deep inner motives for human action, and I would very much like to track them down. If I were able to grasp the hidden psychological links and perhaps, as is my custom, to put it all into a totally fictitious novella, then perhaps I would be satisfied. I know, of course, that my worthy critics – some, not all of them – would be motivated by this to get on their high horse and, in their most sanctimonious manner, condemn me, or to curse me threefold as one who flirts with crime. These people, to whom everything human is quite alien, I am unable to satisfy. They must needs criticise, and although occasionally they inflict considerable pain on me, I grant that they have their role by the wisdom of the Creator. A wagon does need brakes; they are absolutely essential. When occasionally I hear cars squeal pitifully as the brakes are applied, a kind of sympathy steals over me. It does hurt miserably whenever one is suddenly and ruthlessly stopped in full flight. One's interior temperature rises and one needs to be very careful that one does not burst into flame.

What is it that constantly urges me to lift the veil, to look into the causes, to study character, to grasp something I've seen and share it with others, and to inflict it on them despite the fact that it usually earns me blows from behind but neither honour nor money?

It appears to me that God himself is to blame for it. He has, it seems to me now, always led me specifically in that direction, has always pointed with His holy finger and said "There, look!" Obediently I looked, and what I saw formed impressions in me; they grew and urged me irresistibly to give them expression. I was compelled and still am. That is the categorical imperative as I sense it in me.

* * * *

How wonderfully the Lord has led me!

I am the child of poor parents and have seen the hard struggle for a living from my early days. I noted how this struggle was conducted in full consciousness, for my father was extraordinarily well educated although he never had the opportunity to attend a school. I was the youngest in the family. My two brothers grew up ahead of me, attended good schools, and became unusually keen thinkers. The [5] oldest tended to move from theory to practice and in the other the practical outweighed the theoretical. Johann's innermost thoughts often became concrete, practical deeds; Heinrich was able to order concrete facts or figures into wonderful, often profound harmony. My response to them was open-mouthed wonder.

When they debated with Father, who, in the last years of his life sat in a highbacked chair, physically infirm but intellectually alert, I felt dread at the range and the depth of the ideas that were explored. Even then I felt instinctively that it was Father who was always concerned that for his two impetuous sons theory and practice should always be carefully joined.

The more his life sped to its end and the more frail he became physically, the more vigorously he spread about him an atmosphere of a vibrant, genuine, practical piety, full of the joy of life. It was peculiar how the lively young people belonging to the lower, hard-working classes of the population of our home village would prefer to spend time with the old, sick man who was so far above them in education. His education created no gulf between my father and those who were intellectually his inferiors. It helped him understand ordinary people. His piety filled him with love for the least, the simple, and the neglected. His reverent happiness attracted those who longed to escape out of the narrowness and misery of their existence to genuine joy.

When the young folk had departed tears could be seen hesitantly following the deep furrows of my dear father's thin face. He was never a sentimental person; they were tears of joy that he had again felt the warm pulse of life, and that he was privileged to share with some soul or other a fresh drink of unclouded, godly joy that he had himself first tasted.

And my mother? From my father and mother I learned that the husband is the head, but the wife the heart of the family. Without my childlike, godly mother who determined the pulse of our family life, my father too could not have been what he was.

What shall I say about my mother? Oh, I know something which even today brings tears to my eyes, tears of worshipful respect and a boundless, indescribably deep love. Shall I relate this to you? May I relate this to you? Will you refrain from laughing at me?

As a five-year-old I once stood at the knee of my dear mother as she nursed my little sister. [6] Thinking back to that moment, I see a portrait of incomparable beauty with heavenly glory flowing around it: the friendly face of a mother bending over her child which drinks from her heart with unremitting eagerness and never gets enough.

What I received there were impressions. I did not understand what happened, but I felt it all profoundly. That picture accompanies me throughout my life. It was a shining presence and explained for me much better than my teacher could the poem: *"Wenn du noch eine Mutter hast, so danke Gott und sei zufrieden."* [If you still have a mother, thank God, and be content]. My youthful friends often laughed at me because I could never get through that poem without tears.

I once heard my mother say to my father whom she revered: "I feel I am unworthy to offer you a drink of water." Although at that time I had no idea what this metaphorical turn of phrase meant, I immediately knew that this was not a reference to ordinary washing or drinking water. And when Father took Mother's hand in his and said: "Oh yes Mother, you can do precisely that," I again understood intuitively. With internal perception I saw my mother moving about in the family, offering the cleanest, clearest living water from the fountain of her loving heart to anyone who seemed thirsty or tired.

Mother's manner was quite different from Father's. I don't know that any one of her words would have made an especially deep impression on me. But what it was about her that so restored and refreshed us all, and especially my older sister who was always somewhat sickly, consisted not in her words but lay in her inner essence.

At this point I need to insert something about the conditions in our family. I already said that I was the youngest in the family, and then in passing mentioned a younger sister. There were four of us: Johannes, Heinrich, Marie, and yours truly, good-for-nothing Jake. A little sister, born after me, died at the age of three, and so I was again the youngest and was forever being reprimanded. Johannes and Marie have died. Heinrich is still alive and, I am confident, continues his reprimanding with success. What I lack because of the death of brother and sister is now replaced by others with much skill but not as much love.

But more about Father and Mother. Whereas Father's profound wisdom was the bond that enfolded and held the family together, Mother's intimate manner, understanding everything, was the magnet which drew everything to it so that none of us could for any length of time be lost in the distance. Father the head, Mother the heart of the family, and the basis of our [7] blessedness already here on earth, God everything and in all.

While especially Johannes and I have gone on paths of desperate error, our home with its piety and the goodness that flowed from it always ensured that the far country always remained the far country. We could never feel at home out there, and finally found our way back, not only to our earthly home, but especially to the fatherly heart of God.

What a blessing it is to have kind, godfearing parents! Do you, children, quite grasp that today? Are you, parents, even now conscious of it? You fathers, do you always remember that as head of the family it is your obligation in the wisdom which is obedient to God to spin the cord that holds the family together?

And if you hang your head and say: "Alas, I am not as wise as your father was," I take my place beside you and say: "Nor am I."

Now both of us are sad for we know the responsibility we bear for our children. And we can find no comfort for our sorrow anywhere other than in the precious Word of God. It has the advantage over all human comforters in that it comforts us for that which is within, for there especially lies the pain. That both of us are so unwise is our own fault and not that of others. We turn to James 1:5 and read there: "If any of you is lacking in wisdom, ask God, who gives to all generously and ungrudgingly, and it will be given you. But ask in faith, never doubting, for the one who doubts is like a wave of the sea, driven and tossed by the wind." We have also read the sixth verse, fall on our knees and pray: "Dear Lord, I believe; help my unbelief!" Is not that also in the Bible somewhere? And what did the Lord say in response? Read Mark 9:24-29. He answered not in words, but by a deed. He liberated the son of the fearful father from the influences of the evil spirit, a spirit that could be driven out only by prayer and fasting.

He will also draw our children onward as he gives us the true wisdom to be guides and leaders for them. Let us arise from our knees, dear brother, and may we be guides and leaders to our children for their true happiness by faith in our Lord and Master who can do all things.

You, mothers, do you remember that you shape your home with light and warmth so that your child in the far country will dream of nothing but the friendliness [8] and intimacy of home? Are you the warmly beating heart of your family from which flows the clear life-giving spring of living water, from which your loved ones may always drink new strength? Have you become sad over this question? Look up! Did not Jesus first speak to a woman about living water? And did not this woman who began to believe drink from this water? And did not that spring begin to flow in her so that the whole town came to Jesus?

I am a man and can therefore not really understand you in your womanliness. But I know a man who understands you fully and completely. He did what you also do, and as well. He took the children on His lap, hugged them, kissed them, and blessed them. Mothers, open your hearts wide that His light may spread in you. Your worth in your family is determined not by what you say or do but by what you are. Your blessing will build houses for the children you love so much.

* * * *

How short is golden childhood! How short the time of living under the influence of father and mother alone!

It is so warm and bright in the room, and so pleasant to sit in it. Suddenly an Invisible One tears open the door and the icy cold wind of winter invades the room. The Invisible One stands near the door with inexorable, stern face. No one would dare to take his hand off the doorhandle and close the door again.

"Out!" The command is hard and irrevocable. Father understands it first and yields to it. Mother is nearly in despair. A painful whimper rises from her breast. A sword pierces her soul. But she can do nothing. She has to let it happen. The boy knows that the command concerns him. Swaying, he walks past father and mother with uncertain step out into the cold winter of the far country.

Who is this inexorable Invisible One? He is called life, destiny, our evil fate, hard necessity and many another name. But we should not misjudge this Power. It is the Lord. He has never left us in uncertainty over what it means to follow him. "Go from your country and from your kindred and from your father's house to a land that I will show you . . . ." [9] "Whoever loves father or mother more than me is not worthy of me." "The Son of Man has nowhere to lay his head." "Whoever desires to follow me let him deny himself and take up his cross and follow me!" "Be a sojourner in this land . . . ." "Do not think that I have come to bring peace on earth. I have not come to bring peace, but a sword."

Chapter 2

Journey to a Far Country

[9] The icy wind of the far country first hit me when my father became the manager of the Vladimirov *Forstei*.[1] I was a small boy among men who were at the crossroads between youth and adulthood. How different they all were from each other, some so good, and others so bad! That is when I first felt that life was struggle, and only too often I allowed myself to be drawn into the battle.

Through constant association with adults I became very inquisitive and a discomfort to those in the forestry service; to their annoyance I understood more of their conversation than they thought proper. They wanted to be rid of me and some of them did it by giving me a thrashing when I appeared on the scene. They knew that by this behaviour they hurt both me and my parents. I became aware of this double intention very soon, amd became concerned that my parents should not know about these occasional thrashings.

---

[1] One of the forestry camps where Mennonite young men worked as an alternative to military service.

However, I became hardened through this brutality, and became coarse myself. I remember battles in which I, an eight-year-old, would not yield, even though I was beaten up by fellows twenty-one and over who seemed to take pleasure in beating a child; I would not cry but defended myself in a rage, and as soon as my hands were free would attack again. I was then possessed of a devilish rage, and I would have allowed myself to be killed before giving up. The more thoughtful among the service men would then intervene and remove me from those coarse fellows who seemed to take pleasure not only in my physical pain, but also my spiritual trouble.

Even today, when I sense that a wrong has been done me, that rage threatens to rise in me again. I have a hard struggle to wrestle it down. If I am not always anxiously careful to remain in the presence of Christ it wins over me, and then my wrath does what is not right before God.

Certainly I do not wish to blame others for my vices. God has placed me in the struggle so that in His power I will learn to overcome. Perhaps it is a product of those days [10] that I don't quickly get depressed about injustices done me. I am used to it from the days of my youth. Certainly it is God's work that I was shown early what my weakness is.

Still, can we not learn a lesson from the story just told about the danger of giving offence? Perhaps these experiences of childhood help us understand why Jesus spoke so sternly about those through whom offence comes into the world. Offence there will be, but . . . . May we never forget the word spoken by Eternal Love: "It would be better for that person that a millstone be hung around his neck and he be drowned in the sea where it is deepest." Whoever becomes an offence to children is Satan's sower and plants the seeds of the curse in the innocent hearts of those about whom Jesus said: "To them belongs the kingdom of heaven." They rob the child of the kingdom and plant hell in its place. Pay attention to this, all of you who are on the border between youth and adulthood. Whomever it may concern, pay attention!

It was on the *Forstei* that I first began to know loneliness. I was no longer understood. I could not get along with other children very well since I had no experience in that. I could not associate with the adults since I was a child. Father and Mother were always so busy that they had no time for me. I did get that time again when they were old and ailing and the world no longer needed them. Then, as the youngest in the family, I had them again all to myself. At that point I experienced once more with full awareness a time of blessed childhood. I cannot thank my God enough for this.

I was a loner, and during the years on the *Forstei* I wandered about in forest and field. I found that trees, grass and flowers, sun, moon and stars could understand me well and were good company. They were always there for me, and they were never dead things to me. They shared with me their wonderful life. In fact, I suspect that they are the ones who taught me to "lie,"[2] which even today fills my critics with such horror.

God be praised that the stones cry out when man is silent; that the creation comforts even when the lords of creation misuse and wound.

* * * *

I was seven years old when for the first time I had to leave my home, which was then the Vladimirov *Forstei*. I boarded with strangers and went to school with children I did not know. But I always went home for Saturday and Sunday. I took a somewhat superior attitude to my new friends, a result of my boundless pretentiousness. [11] I was, however, a better than average student. For example, I do not remember when I learned to read and write. I could always do that, and when I first went to the public school as a beginner, I actually began with the third grade and during that year moved to grade four. I was seated just ahead of the most advanced student in the small school. During the arithmetic period I turned around when he was not looking, copied his exercises with fractions, and easily solved them. When he became aware of what I was doing, I got my first beating in school. However, what was that in comparison to what I had already experienced at the *Forstei*? I was not even angry at this lout. At that point something much more serious made its way into my heart; it was contempt.

---

[2] He means the imagination of the fiction he was given to writing.

This vice also is to this day a thorn in my flesh. When rage overcomes me it also passes away again quickly. But once I begin to have contempt for a person, I am in for a long, hard struggle with pride and lovelessness before I can overcome and I am once more able to respect and love that brother. Without Jesus I could never do it.

My time in school without father or mother in the cold, far country was and remained a difficult time for me. To all of that was added that the lady who provided my meals died before I had half finished my first year. I can hardly remember her, but the night of her death haunts me with inexorable clarity. Awakened from a restless sleep, I saw the skeletal body of the woman who had just died stretched out on a bench under a white sheet in the big room.[3] Beyond the body, it seemed to me, was death grinning at me. I had seen death represented as a skeleton in books, but in this night for the first time, I saw his frightful majesty, terrifyingly near, spreading his dark wings with empty indifference over the dead woman and her weeping family, cold and without heart. I wanted to see no more, and with unspeakable fear I buried my head in the pillow. From then on I experienced a spine-chilling fear when darkness fell and I had to go to bed. Often, bathed in the sweat of fear, I lay awake until after midnight, and then finally called to those who were in the room. They scolded me for the disturbance, but at the sound of that human voice I went to sleep. No matter that it was a scolding; the human sound broke the silence of the night and its ghostly, eerie darkness, and so took away its fearfulness. The pitiless Invisible One had called me out into the cold, far country when I was merely seven years old. Rage, contempt, and the fear of death attempted to push into my heart and be my steady companions. If God, the dear [12] Heavenly Father had not provided a counterweight, who knows where I would be today?

However, in that cold, far country I also found enough warm love to pull me back from the precipice. First, I wish to say "thank you" to my foster-sister from that time. I believe she is still alive and perhaps now even in Canada. I don't know how she was to me what she was. I only remember how comforting it was for me when we sat on the short bench

---

[3] The "große Stube," the standard living room in every Russian Mennonite house.

in the chimney corner in the small room and talked to each other. What we said was so unimportant that I remember not a word of it, but it was the expression of the love children have for each other. How pleasant it was when we sat together in the dark kitchen in front of the open fire. It was from here that the oven which heated the living room was fired with straw. The straw fire was burning in the stove. Tina took a large handful of straw and put it into the mouth of the glowing oven. Everything around us became dark and mysterious and quiet. We held our breath and listened. Immediately near us the dark mystery of the night pressed upon us, but being near Tina, who was a few years older than I, I was not afraid of the night. The light would return again. Now it began to crackle in the oven and the first flames licked at the straw. Hesitantly, the mysterious darkness began to recede from us. I saw Tina's face light up in the red glow of the fire, and then the flame shot up and the whole kitchen was bright as day. Only in the far corners of the house the darkness was still lurking and tried to make me afraid. "Just wait until you are in bed! Then I will cover you! Then you will be mine to frighten and torture!" But there was still time before that. For now I was sitting in Tina's safe presence. What did I care that Tina's older brothers called me a "girls' boy?" I was no longer offended by it. I had endured far worse than that. And Tina comforted me so that I forgot the teasing, but her words I do not remember. They were, however, kind, friendly words which gave me peace.

The dark night of being alone also could not long frighten me. My widowed host understood the small scared boy and put my bed next to his. Because of this the place where the dead woman had lain was much closer to me than before, but uncle[4] Warkentin often could not go to sleep for a long time, and did not scold me when I called to him. He answered me with his kind, somewhat sad voice, and then the night was no longer so terrifying. In time that sinister terror quite disappeared, and I could climb into my snug bed again without fear.

In school there was also someone who loved me. It was my teacher, then a very young but now an old man, who [13] is also now in Canada

---

[4] Uncle is here used as a term of respect, not of relationship.

somewhere trying under straitened circumstances to make a living. I can tell you less today about what he taught me, than about what he was to me at that time when cold night reached for my soul in order to suffocate it in wrath, contempt and fear. I believe that a major advantage of our schools there [in Imperial Russia] was that their primary purpose was the total upbringing of the children. For that reason the teacher's importance consisted not so much in what he could do but in what he was, not what he taught but what he lived. Nor did that system in any way deprive us of the required general knowledge.

From my teacher P.K. I received exactly two blows, and they were very painful for me. Not physically. My goodness, they were administered with a stick that was already cracked and even so without any force. But it hurt in my heart. I did not understand, but I sensed that the blows hurt my teacher, whom I revered, and never after that did I knowingly grieve him. My impertinence and whatever other excessive behaviour still adhered to me may, of course, have caused him some difficult hours.

Thus world and love struggled for me, and love was so strong and beautiful that it won. Nor did I lose my faith in love later when I encountered a teacher from whom I learned much but received little for my inner life. There was a kind of complementarity between him and me; I earned the thrashings, and he administered them with a thoroughness that left nothing to be desired.

I always remained a "girls' boy." Apart from wandering astray a few times, I remain happy about it. The girls have always been a blessing for me. Perhaps that is why I later became a "girls' teacher." Could Liesa and Susa Nikkel still be alive somewhere in the wide world? These two were the neighbour girls and they were frequently witnesses to my arguments with that teacher, which usually ended with the empirical proofs of a beating. Things were not quiet on those occasions because I had the impertinence to defend myself. Once the procedure was over and I came back to the house, a pair of blue and a pair of brown eyes greeted me over the fence. They enticed me and I could not resist. Defying the danger that I would again be ridiculed as a "girls' boy" by my friends, I went over.
"Did he beat you again?"

"Yes."
"Why?"
"Oh, you know."
"Did it hurt a lot?"
"Yes."
"Did you cry?"
"Not a bit. Just to make him mad." [14]
"Will he beat you again?"
"Yes."
"You want to eat some lentils?"

In the back of Nikkel's garden grew the best and sweetest lentils I have ever tasted in my life. Susa ran off and asked her mother whether we could go and eat lentils and got permission. And those sweet lentils bore away my pains. It was not difficult to comfort me since my pains were, sad to say, only physical and nothing more. Oh, they were dark times then, but they were transfigured by the love which beamed at me from one pair of blue and one pair of brown eyes and which I tasted in those sweet lentils. It may be that I owe more to those lentils, which I then devoured by the spoonful, than to the wisdom of the school.

The time came for me when I tried to form ties with my schoolmates, but could not manage it. My heart hungered for friendship and I could not find it. I suspected that what prevented it was the occasion of the teasing I had endured, and I tried to leave it behind. I stopped resolutely being a "girls' boy" and began to run with the respected big boys. They, however, judged that I was too soft for their undertakings and perhaps too much of a goody-goody, and so I tried to be coarse and naughty in order to gain their favour. But it did no good. They took advantage of me, lured me into traps they set for me and then, very unfairly, left me sitting in them. Often I found myself holding the bag for others. Rarely was I called by my name; always only by a nickname. That lasted until I entered the last year of the Secondary School in Gnadenfeld.

I can see that rejection today as a blessing. It showed me that the love of the world cannot be bought for there is no such thing. The world will always offer us stones instead of bread even if for one moment's bliss we were to surrender our souls to her and choke out whatever was noble and good in us. I turned my back on that world. Certainly I waded through depths of sin later, but I have never been able to make peace with the world. I no longer trusted her. And that helped me in a decisive moment so that the return to God was not difficult.

* * * *

My last and only year in the Secondary School at Gnadenfeld was one of the happiest of my life. Whether my teachers enjoyed me as much as I them, is an open question. I had brought with me from my earlier life much that they were required to prune and cut away. The striving for friendship with those who were regarded as [15] the most popular no longer stood between me and the teachers. I sought my teachers and found them. No doubt I was always a burden to them, no longer because of deliberate and calculated contrariness, but because of the insufferable pretentiousness in which, without any justification, I occasionally thought myself to be superior to everything. But my teachers tolerated that as well with a smile and without resentment.

What I no longer sought, I now found: good, faithful friends. There were thirteen of us in the class, and these thirteen are one of the weighty reasons why I do not regard thirteen as an unlucky number. We thirteen really were a unit, a whole, that held together in joy and sorrow, both in striving for the great ideals as well as in drinking lemonade and eating halvah, at which the strictest of our teachers, W.P. Neufeld, who died in Reedley, California, caught us redhanded. I was startled by the trembling of his refined nostrils which I noticed while he gave us a reprimand without ever raising his voice even a shade. I thought the trembling was caused by his barely-controlled anger, and we feared his wrath. But there was another reason for it. I had a small suspicion that evening during the interrogation. It revealed that because of this evening's party, I had been unfaithful in my duty, which was to make the rounds of the east end of the village as night watchman. Teacher Neufeld lectured me very earnestly about my dereliction of duty. However, the crow's feet in the corners of his eyes became more and more pronounced and suddenly his severity appeared to me to be so friendly that all my fear dissipated. He, however, adhered to the principle that a penalty was necessary. This time, too, he did not betray his principle, although I no longer remember what the penalty was. It was probably not severe, but nonetheless effective.

It also happened that, as a group, we opposed our teachers and argued with them. This never happened to cover over or deny some meanness on our part, but always to defend a real or imagined right. The teachers always responded with seriousness and treated us as adults. Frequently, of course, it turned out in these arguments over rights that we were in the wrong, whereupon we accepted the disputed rules. Only our Russian teacher, poor G.S., was once vanquished and had to give in because, in his anger, he had insulted us with hurtful words. [16]

It happened this way. We had a friend in the class whom we all liked very much and about whom we did not know whether he was first or thirteenth among us. There was nothing average about him, but something extreme in his appearance and demeanour which could locate him only at one of the ends. We had given him the nickname Tips and there was a specific reason for it. His name was Loewen. In Gnadenfeld there was a certain man named Toews who had married the daughter of a Loewen family and who, in order to distinguish him from other Loewens, was called Loewen's Toews. What else could we do but transfer this name to our friend Loewen? A person who is loved often has many names. However, over time this long name became too cumbersome. One of us commented that the use of the long name took too much time, especially during the short winter days. So the Loewen part of the name was scrapped and only Toews remained. Since, however, that same Loewen, alias Loewen-Toews, alias Toews was quite rotund in shape, the name gradually changed from Toews to Tips, and that was his name as long as we talked about him.

Tips was capable of quite unpredictable pranks, and for this reason he had his seat on the front bench immediately under the surveillance of the teacher. The bell had sounded for the geography period to begin. We were awaiting the teacher G.S. At the reading desk directly in front of Tips and towering over him stood the class assistant, the broad-shouldered H.R. the Second, preparing the chalk for the teacher. The teacher did not arrive. Tips looked up at R.'s broad back, got up slowly, stepped onto the front bench and waited. Still the teacher did not come.

Tips stepped onto the teacher's desk. It was high time for the teacher to arrive but still he did not come. Tips looked quickly toward the door which remained stubbornly closed, and then climbed up on R.'s broad shoulders, and crooked his left arm at his side like a proud horseman. His mount bore the load effortlessly, but seemed unwilling to respond to the encouraging calls of the rider to get going. "Come on!" Tips called in a low voice, and fidgeted about with his short legs to indicate that he was giving the spurs to the flanks of his mount. At that moment the door opened and teacher G.S. made his entrance. Tip's strong horse made a slight movement with his shoulders towards the right and down, a kind of bucking [17] motion, and the rotund, daring horseman rolled down to the feet of the indignant teacher, a small heap of misery.

What a drama! Tips and H.R. were ordered up to stand in the aisle in front of the desk. Teacher G.S. sat there, his head down, hands folded on his desk, chewing grimly on his lower lip. Dead silence. My neighbor, the fidgety G.V. who bore the honourary title of *Trieschka*, began to move back and forth on his seat, for the situation seemed so comical to him that he threatened to burst as he tried to contain his laughter. And then the misfortune; he snorted out in laughter. If only one could reconstruct that indefinable but characteristic sound! "Pffchrrrpch-ha-ha-ha . . ." The furious eyes of the teacher looked right through the offender, who was laughing quite helplessly and trying without success to regain control over himself. The teacher looked daggers at him but to no avail. V. could not stop laughing, and a few other faces were struggling for control by now. Such hearty laughter is infectious. A furious "Durrrrack!" ["Idiot!"] finally exploded from the teacher's desk. That did it for the others as well. Very angry people have no idea how comical they appear to others and the more comical they are, the more they rant and rave. Loud laughter, many-voiced, greeted the teacher's furious outburst. But now G.S. could no longer stand it. He jumped up from his chair, the floodgates of his eloquence opened and this same teacher, who could read to us so soulfully from the artistic treasures of Russian literature that we forgot time and place, let loose on us a flood of abusive insults. It was his unfortunate character. He was no more able to control his violent temper than G.V. his laughter. What he said to us was so venomous and insulting that we were abruptly quiet and became very sober. At that point teacher G.S. realized that he had lost control and restrained himself.

There was no geography that day. The teacher left the class insulted, but also – and that is to his credit – ashamed. He was a man of deep feeling, and his moods changed at the drop of a hat. We, however, were too stupid to feel sorry for a man who bears his torturer with him in the shape of his own unhappy character. We found no mitigating circumstance for [18] the insults which the teacher had flung at us, guilty or not, and we were determined to have our revenge. But we arrived at this decision without including Tips. In our view, he had caused this wretchedness with his mischief. And we did not care to remember at this moment that we had often taken such delight in his pranks when they did not end as tragically as this one – that we liked him especially as our comedian. Our dear friend did not resent being left out.

We felt quite important for having been insulted, for we had justice on our side, and those who know they are right always feel important, much too important. It was in the assurance of our importance that we decided on revenge.

Teacher G.S.'s next period came. He entered, took his seat at his desk, opened the book, and asked with somewhat embarrassed and guilty friendliness, "How far had we come, gentlemen?" That we were now suddenly gentlemen did not strike us as in the least comical. We were in the top grade and we were in the right, why should we not be gentlemen? He addressed us that way quite seriously and that is the way we accepted it, as something that was our due. No one responded. "Gentlemen, will you not tell me where we left off in the last hour?" No answer. Teacher G.S. certainly realized by this time that he was dealing with a regular strike. He snapped the book shut and gravely addressed us: "Gentlemen, I did not think that you would take revenge, particularly since you know that it was because of your misbehaviour that I became so agitated as to do you wrong." That should have been more than enough, but of course we were right, and so we began to accuse the poor man over everything he had said to us. He was big enough to take it and before long we began to feel ashamed of ourselves. I don't quite know how the matter would have ended gracefully had not Tips appeared on the scene as a helper in distress. When the situation was becoming really embarrassing, he rose with outrage all over his face and addressed the teacher with these classic words: "Yes, and you said I deserved to be beaten with a stick and that I was a pest." The day was saved. Teacher G.S. recovered his confidence, and with a smile on his lips said, "Loewen, I say with my hand on my heart: you are a real pest, and a beating with a stick could only do you good." [19] Relief settled over the whole class. Loewen turned to us slowly and said in Low German: "*Doa, von mi lat he sich nuscht saje.*" [There you are; he won't take anything from me]. The teacher did not hear what he said, but suspected his meaning and did not take offence. "You sit down and be quiet! Now, lads, how far did we get in the last hour?" Now that we were boys again and not gentlemen, things were back to comfortable normality and the lesson took its course. But we had won, and for a long time we basked in the sunshine of that glory.

Where are they all, those who basked in that sunshine? Of the teachers only one survives, and life is not going well for him. (He has since also died.) And my friends?

Tips is likely still suffering in a Russian prison because he became a preacher of the gospel.

G.V. is a missing person.[5]

H.E. died long ago.

G.D. became a doctor and, although he had a heart ailment, was carried off by the imperial government to Odessa, where he succumbed to a heart attack. He was sent home in a casket.

H.R. the First still lives and may sooner or later be able to come to Canada.

H.R. the Second died of typhus during the war.

---

[5] The word is *verschollen*. It means that he was taken away by force during the revolutionary troubles and was not heard from again.

H.K. is tormented in a position whose demands he cannot reconcile with his conscience.

J.H. has for more than thirty years been the model of a faithful teacher in the same village – that is, if the Reds have not driven him away.

H.N. was betrayed and murdered.

A.H. was attacked on the road and murdered.

J.H. lives in Russia under difficult circumstances.

D.B. died of typhus during the war.

And number thirteen sits here and writes his memoirs.

All were my good friends. God be with the living! Quiet rest to the dead! Peace to their ashes!

Chapter 3

Between the Dark Shadow of Sin
and the Bright Beams of Love

A beautiful, brief year, a year in which again I had my parents all to myself. They had had to retire, and now had more time to live for their family and their little circle of friends. It was during this time that I [20] marvelled again and again at my father's conversations with my older brothers. But it was only a single, short, wonderful year. Then I was compelled to begin my active participation in the hard struggle of life, of which I had been aware since my early years.

Father had never been stingy and that is also why he was always poor. But neither had he borrowed, and consequently he remained a free man all his life. He wanted to die as a free man. One day, well before the school year had ended he called me and put to me the question: "What now?" He never doubted that I would pass the matriculation examination. He had helped me up to that point, but now, in chronic ill health, he could no longer do anything for me. The small farm which we owned and the paint business in which he was still active, did not earn enough to pay for any further education for me. As for me, I had developed a taste for learning and would have loved to continue, but ....

Father had rich acquaintances and even "patrons." Should we turn to them for help? "And supposing they help us," said father, "I cannot shoulder the responsibility for the debt we should incur. That would become your burden." I understood everything perfectly, but the choice and the decision were very difficult for me. I could say nothing and likely looked at my father with tears in my eyes which was very unusual for me.

One day some very unusual letters arrived. My father had betrayed his principles and had turned to his patrons for help toward my education. However, the letters brought negative responses from those "protectors". There is in fact a problem with these "protectors." Generally they are very benevolent, but they rarely grant much to you, except to let you become a social ornament for them. At that point I had a small intuition about the soil in which socialist hate flourished. But my father took quite a different view of the matter. He stood up straight and said: "A man has to stand on his own two feet!" Then he turned to me and said, "Can you get on without them, or shall we go on begging?" "Never that," I answered, more in rage than with determination, for I could not yet surrender what was so dear to me. I could say nothing as yet about my further plans, for once a word had been spoken in our house, it stood.

I did not want to become a teacher. Never. Nor could I afford to begin farming on our small holding[1] which barely supported our aging parents. [21] I was determined to become a marine engineer regardless of the cost. If however, I took life as it actually was, all the lines converged to a single point. Immediately after the end of school I had to begin earning some money. But only one possibility lay open. I had just turned sixteen and had therewith reached the age at which, according to Russian law, I could become a teacher. Given my brashness and the ease with which I learned, it was entirely possible for me to do private study and be ready by the autumn to pass the teacher's examinations in the district town. It was the only way any of us could see. But I did not wish to go that way.

---

[1] Farmsteads in the Mennonite villages had initially been quite large, almost 200 acres in size. However, changes in state legislation in the mid-nineteenth century made it possible for Mennonites to divide these lands into much smaller parcels; some barely larger than the buildings themselves. Janzen's family lived on such a "small farm."

It was twilight on one of the first warm days of spring in the year 1894. I came out of the little wood behind our garden where I had been doing my homework. The windows of our house stood wide open. Quietly I approached and sat down on the bench that stood under Father's window just to watch the sunset. I felt that pleasant languor which spring warmth can bring. Inside, I heard someone sigh. It was the sigh from Mother's heart and I knew it well. It was that sigh which was wrung from her whenever she believed she had to give someone a drink while all the fountains in her had run dry. For a moment there was silence. Then I heard Father say, "If only I could get the boy out of this mind-set!" There they sat, together, and were concerned not for me but about me. They had already had enough of the burden and heat of the day. They had a right, if anyone had, to rest and be supported by those whom they had brought this far by toil and effort, never thinking of themselves. I was ashamed of myself. Quietly I got up and tiptoed around the house so that my parents would not notice that I had been eavesdropping. I entered the house through the back door. I waited briefly in the small room. Mother was just lighting Father's lamp and I wanted to step into its light. First I had to get control of my facial expression so that it would not betray to my parents any dissatisfaction or displeasure. I was determined to take the concerns they had about me on myself, and that they should have no occasion to feel sorry for me. I would have to do it with good humour.

I don't know what my face betrayed as I stepped into the big room, but it must have been somewhat peculiar because father looked at me for a drawn-out moment and said, "What's up?" [22] A face that attempts to be happy when it should actually be crying no doubt looks peculiar. Besides, it is hard to deceive one's parents about what one is feeling intensely. Mother stopped her knitting and looked at me with incomprehension. As for me, I first had to swallow hard several times, a painful smile on my lips, before I was able to express what I had come to say. But it was imperative; I had to say it, and it had to be said firmly, with courage and with cheerfulness. However, the hesitation in the little room ripped my concentration to shreds again, and once more I had to gain control with new effort. I expect that with my preparations to speak I must have looked like a beginner in Sunday school who is about to appear before an audience for the first time to recite a poem. But finally I did say it: "You know what, Papa and Mama? I can become a teacher." And then a sensation flooded over me which I always felt over there in Russia when the gravediggers had finished, laid their shovels over the grave mound, and stepped back. *Finita la commedia.* [The comedy has ended].

And now the time for play was over. I stood in the middle of the struggle of life. I was lamenting my first great sacrifice in this struggle. I had had to retreat, and therewith began my battle. But I retreated only for a new attempt to advance, and this retreat with which my battle began made me fully aware that I was no longer being carried by others but that I was personally confronting life. As my thoughts came and went, I became more self-confident and hopeful. It had to work; it would work. I did not know at the time – or at least I did not think of it then nor for some time afterwards – that an almighty hand had guided me onto a life-long path on which work and struggle awaited me, to be sure, but also much pure and genuine joy.

I must omit much of importance here. Perhaps I can tell it later sometime. Today, it is the simultaneous conflicts and their combined influence on me that rise before me. In September, 1894, I did indeed pass the teacher's examinations in the district city of Melitopol. Personal luck, my intellectual quickness, and my audacity all contributed beautifully to the result. My dear fellow-student Bernhard, who was older and always more mature than I, but who was never able to rise to my level of audacity, simply ran away when it appeared to him that he had not solved a mathematical problem correctly. I did not care a whit when I found out that in my written work I had discoursed on attributive rather than on objective sentences, and [23] I went to the next examination as though I could not lose. What the timid pen had spoiled, the nimble tongue set right; I received my diploma and was engaged as assistant teacher in Rudnerweide [a village about 10 km from Gnadenfeld]. Thus far everything had come together wonderfully. But now came the conflicts. Wherever do I begin with that?

* * * *

What had always saved me in my hours of need was the love I experienced. That year in Gnadenfeld was transfigured for me by the love of my parents, the love of friends, and not to forget it, genuine, flaxen-haired adolescent love, which, however, never led to engagement. Nevertheless, it did me a lot of good. The lasses of Gnadenfeld were well brought up and would tolerate no questionable behaviour. However, I enjoyed their favour and I was careful not to squander their goodwill. I loved being in their presence and to visit with them, to moan in love over one of them, and even to look at her languidly, but not too obviously. In hours of special favour I sat near her in the little arbour in Rempel's garden to tease her. I simply could not get on without that. This impertinence is strong and demands expression; the fox finally has to come out of the hole. I did not dare to touch her, but now and again I established a material link, if only an intermediate one, between us; I held the cotton thread which she was busily crocheting. I am sure I can not patent this procedure, for I can hardly claim to be its inventor. I have read about it in novels and have also observed that earlier generations used this method of linking to good effect.

Later, alas, this linking sometimes proved to be too weak to prevent sexual temptations from coming upon me. Still, once when I was in real peril, I felt a tugging at that thread, and I could not consent.

This adolescent love followed me out into the battle of life along with the love of my parents and it was a blessing to me. May God be thanked! For all love comes from Him. The fact that love is sometimes serious, sometimes merry, even mischievous, and sometimes comical, proves nothing to the contrary. What is divine about love is that it always blesses, whatever its form.

The demonic aspect of lust is that it always yields a curse. That is why I am so sorry for the youth of today who know so much more than we did and can be entirely blasé at the age of sixteen. They laugh at that kind of love, and therefore do not experience it. But they are helpless victims of [24] lust. If only the youth of today could grasp that cotton thread! They would be much happier for it. However, I am becoming discouraged. Only too easily does one grow beyond that "cotton thread," but one can never return to it. What is past is gone. The educators of today load themselves with guilt because they give the poison fruit of the Tree of Knowledge even to children.

In Rudnerweide I found new friends, faithful ones whom I remember with pleasure. But I also got into bad company. I don't quite know how it happened. It is one of the contradictions of life, for I never felt good in the filth of sin. Nor can I say that I was led into sin as a weak one in that company. Rather, I occasionally felt that there was a kind of pleasure in advancing along the road of wickedness. The Catholic priest says in his book *Das Volk von Neusorge* [The People of Neusorge] concerning his ordination to the priesthood: "I always hear, and to this day I hear with pain, the word in my soul: *segregatus a populo* (separated from the people)." Can it be that as an eighteen-year-old I already felt something similar in my soul?

I have always been angry when people who were not farmers spoke of the "stupid farmer." We have come from and belong to a people who are Mennonite farmers, even if we are the most famous professors in the world which, alas, we have not yet become. And some who are and for that reason have left our people, have done themselves great harm by it. This I have always thought and felt. And should we grow beyond a certain *niveau* and not be understood by most of our people, our love and our work should still be for them, for it gives us a basis on which we can grow and develop, and from which we can rise to a height and uniqueness which in time will be acknowledged. Whoever has reached such a level should always unselfishly hold out a hand to his people, whether he be recognized for his achievements or not. *Segregatus a populo.*

I am no Catholic priest, but there are those who have been constantly offended because I liked the company of the little people, indeed even those whose reputations were somewhat tarnished, such as horse traders and others like that. I regret that sometimes I agreed to what was not right, but I do not regret that I lived their humble life with the humble and certainly do not accuse them of having led me astray. Rather, I did not do my duty with respect to them, for I could distinguish good from evil better than those with whom I waded through the depths of sin. [25] I knew more and therefore I was also responsible for more. They did not lead me astray, but I neglected to make them aware of the danger of the road they had taken. I do not regret that I have been with my people and I would rather be with them than anywhere else.

True, I had to experience a *segregatio a populo* for God's sake when he called me into his royal priesthood and made me to be born again to an imperishable hope. Here too I say with the words of my Catholic mentor: "Only in the sense of transformation and being transfigured, only as death toward a new life could I accept the *segregatio a populo*." Although sin is an abomination to me and although I see the sin of my people and do not want to be part of it but rather to flee from it, nevertheless I still stand by my people. My work is for my people regardless of whether they praise or despise me.

Therefore, my dear friends, who cannot understand why again and again I expose my innermost heart and let the people trample it, let me go my way, for I am compelled to go it. From this people I have come, and in this people my children must stand if they are to be preserved and not sink to become a colourless nobody. That is why I need always to give this people the best that I have. That is my innermost conviction.

I give my best to my people and in doing so in no way throw pearls before swine. I cannot prevent swine who come along from trampling on what they find. If they disregarded Christ's work, why should they honour mine? Anything good in what I do will find its echo and bear fruit. I sow the word. God must provide rain and blessing, growth and prosperity. If He has sent me to sow, no doubt He will have prepared the field, even though I may not always recognize it.

* * * *

And so my life moved between the dark shadow of sin and the bright beams of love. The beams of love came from warm, friendly hearts who did not break faith with me even though I might have deserved it. Until now I had quite overlooked them and held them in slight regard. They were the children, my pupils.

I did not deserve that love of the children. Perhaps something in my nature attracted them, especially the little ones. I did not fare so well with the older ones. In my high-spirited youthfulness and in my pride that I had a position and was financially independent, I never let them forget that I was their teacher although they were only a scant two years younger than

I. [26] Actually things went better with the older students than would have seemed possible under such circumstances. I'm surprised that things went so well. Whatever they did to me, it was not enough to spoil my joy in my work with the little ones.

Actually it is a bit exaggerated to speak of *work* with the little ones. It seems to me that everything which at that time could be called work was an offence to me. What was work then, as I recall it, was the correction of writing exercises and dictations. Everything else was play, heartwarming, happy, interesting play. In the religion period we studied the *Biblische Geschichten* [Bible Stories] by Ludwig Wangemann. I told the stories, always keeping close to the words of the book. The book was written in the venerable language of Luther's Bible translation so that even the little ones could easily understand them. The children listened with the attention born of curiosity; I did not have to coerce them to it with my stern manner. Children love stories, and attention is natural. Then we discussed the story we had read. How the little ones participated!

Peter shook both of his little fists and exclaimed, "Oh, that Cain was a bad one! I'd paste him one!" Little Tina answered, "Then you'd be just as bad as Cain himself. He always had to hit someone. But Abel was so good. Why ever did God let Cain kill him?" There I had it, a really big question. Indeed, why did He allow it? Why did He think of the mark of Cain afterwards, when it was too late? Why had I yielded to the temptation to tell the children a story which Wangemann had kept for later, and which now threw up such a question? Earlier, during the story of the Fall, Tina had expressed her regret that God had not come a *little bit* earlier (she emphasized *little bit* so strongly that her little voice cracked). Then the pair would have been afraid of Him and would not have eaten of the forbidden fruit. It had been easy to deal with that one. After all, I said, Tina did not obey her mother because she was afraid of her but because she loved her and did not want to cause her pain. It had been easy to explain that God wanted the human pair to obey Him out of love and not fear. But now it was much more difficult. Apparently I was silent somewhat too long, because Franz, the precocious one, stood up without raising his hand and said, "God always lets people do everything by themselves." [27] "And then He punishes them," said Marie. I intervened. "How did He punish Cain?" I asked. "He chased him far away." "No, He did not," I said. "He only said that Cain would be a fugitive and a wanderer. But He never said that Cain should go away." There was a lull as the children strained themselves to understand, and I, the big child, no less. "But He made a mark on his forehead," said one. "Yes, but that was only so that no one would kill him," Franz answered for me. "It was not a punishment." "But then why did Cain run away and live in the land of Nod?" asked Marie. Now I got the floor. "It was because he was afraid to live in the place where he had killed his brother."

That made sense, and if the children did not quite grasp it intellectually, they nevertheless felt intuitively that sin can deprive one of house and home even if God never punishes. But the question remained, that God leaves mortals to their own devices, warns them beforehand, and then charges them with the sin. The little ones soon forgot it, but I took the question with me on my obscure, dark ways, and it always admonished me: "God lets you do what you want, but He warns you not to sin, for sin can deprive you of house and home, and after that you must account for it."

Learning the Bible stories was not a task during which we waited impatiently for the recess bell to ring. Reading, memorizing poems, arithmetic; it was all play and pleasure, not hard work. And I was always more the learner than the teacher and did not know it.

* * * *

I always took that admonition with me from school into my life outside. Indeed, one could conclude from the words of the Lord to Cain that it was He, God, who, as Cain later said, drove Cain away from His presence and cursed the earth which had opened its mouth to receive from Cain's hand the blood of his brother. Basic to all that was the terrible sin of fratricide. God had come to Cain and had said that he should rule over sin which lurked before his door, but it had been of no use. It would probably also have done no good at the primal Fall had God arrived a little earlier. No, it is not given to the commandment which, when it is broken brings death, to restrain us from sin. Only patient, longsuffering, inconceivable love can do that.

Even as I thought these thoughts my feet took me out on the paths of darkness. Could not the thoughts stimulated by [28] the lesson of the schoolroom, which God had sent me as a warning, restrain me from these ways? What awful power was it that drew me out irresistibly? And I closed my eyes in the darkness and went – hurried – as though something might prevent my enjoyment.

Tomorrow the sun would shine again. It would shine so brightly that it would fill my classroom with light, even though it faced north and no direct rays would enter it. The bright eyes of children would look to me expectantly like open doors into their pure souls. Clarity, purity, and light would surround me and make their demands upon me.

Would I not have to hide my face and flee from all this light with the complaint of Cain: "You have driven me away this day from Your face and whoever finds me will slay me"? I felt as though huge waves were crashing around me threatening to overwhelm me. I was in the grip of that awesome fear I had known since childhood, but I could not go back. Further and further I was driven on the paths of night. Let me not talk about it. They were terrible years of struggle. I was not the combatant; I was only the prize for the winner. I was the prize of the contest.

Once I sat before my open Bible when, at four in the morning, dawn came again after a night without sleep. "But when the archangel Michael, contending with the devil, disputed about the body of Moses, he did not presume to pronounce a reviling judgement upon him but said, 'The Lord rebuke you!'" [Jude 9] Was it not as though Michael, the archangel, had respect for the awful power of the Lord of darkness? Was it not as though one saw the devil pursue his dark purposes unerringly with refined cunning, purposes whose terrible goal is hidden from us, but which would in time be even more terribly revealed? What was it about the body of Moses? Had it at least been his soul! Of what concern was I to him? Why was God concerned to send His archangel to frustrate the ways of the devil? A battle ensued which forced the archangel to respect his opponent so that he did not dare to condemn him with insulting words, but committed the matter to the Lord. "The Lord rebuke you!" Why was God concerned for me, that He kept sending me His servants in their bright innocence to battle with Satan for me? More and more I recognized the terrible power of sin. More and more I began to understand the words "slavery of sin." [29] Moreover, a presentiment of the light of divine mercy hovered over me. I could not grasp it. I knew everything about Jesus the Saviour. I had believed on Him but I had not yet quite grasped His significance as Saviour, and had not experienced it in its full power because I did not know until then what sin was.

Through the years I had experienced that sin destroys people, and that by its nature it must do so. But even more; I learned that, for me personally, sin with its destructive character was transformed into guilt by my own consent to it. I could not be made responsible for what happened to me without my participation. I could indeed become a victim of sin, but my conscience would remain unburdened. But Satan in his perversity was able so to manipulate me so that, despite my better knowledge, I consented to the sin, and therefore bore the guilt for my own destruction. And then he told me as he had once said to Cain and then later to Judas: "Your sin is too great to be forgiven."

At that point – I had already moved to Pastwa [a village about 20 km east of Gnadenfeld] – I turned my back on sin and my bad company. But I did not turn to God. Before that, another influence was to grip me. I fell victim to the influences of Russian nihilism and came into the company of Russian revolutionaries, although without much enthusiasm.[2] The guilt of sin still weighed on me and would not let me breathe freely. Besides, my eyes were sharp enough to see through the hollow speciousness of the whole thing.

I came to understand the character of my village society one night at a wild drunken party. I learned about the nature of the Russian ideas about the overthrow of existing society and their plans for the happiness of the world on the occasion of a semi-secret meeting of representatives of these

---

[2] Those disillusioned with the state's refusal to initiate serious reform became active in various revolutionary movements from the 1860s on. Young intellectuals were especially attracted to nihilism, which declared that all of society's existing beliefs and values must be destroyed so that a new world could be created. This notion was popularized in Turgenev's celebrated novel, *Fathers and Sons*, published in 1861.

views in a wood near the neighboring village of Licht. There I saw what was hidden under the cloak of noble endeavour. Already during the discussion of current political questions there was something here that was not what it appeared to be. *Chto-to ne to* says the Russian proverb, (something is not what it seems).

Once the more official part of the meeting had been completed, that "something" was revealed without disguise. I saw that these representatives of a noble ideology were slaves of sin, burdened with guilt, and consumed by a corruption of the soul to such a degree that one could not expect any good of any kind from them. The full meaning of the verse from Holy Scripture applied to them: "For it is a shame even to speak of the things that they do in secret" [Eph. 5:12]. In this company, all of this was kept secret from the world which was to be overturned, punished, made better, and who knows what else. But among the enlightened and initiated all of these self-evident and natural things did [30] not need to be kept secret. The *tovarischchi* (comrades) understood each other fully. For a while I sat on a tree stump and listened to their vulgarities. Then I dredged up a hateful, vulgar curse out of the filthy bottom of my own sick soul, flung it in their faces, and walked off. I was empty inside, desolate. Someone who has never experienced it will surely not understand. These are the hours in which one commits suicide, if God's goodness does not watch over one in a special way.

From then on my friends from the village considered me proud since I did not wish to communicate with them any longer. The revolutionaries called me crazy. Neither of their reactions were of any concern to me.

* * * *

My school now occupied my whole life. There was a lot of sunshine there, and in the schoolroom I still found the love of children, although it was not as general as it had been in Rudnerweide. Now and again, in the classroom among the children, I was able to become really enthusiastic, but it was temporary. Actually I did not make much progress in my work but I had not really noticed it as long as I was drifting on the current of sin and the world. Now that I had isolated myself I noticed how much was lacking, how much had been neglected, and I wanted to make up for it. But I took hold of the wrong end. More and more I exercised my authority against my pupils and tried to force them to work, even as I tried to coerce myself to do the good. God saved me at that time from death by the light and love in my school, but I no longer recognized the powers that could liberate me, and I knew even less from whom these powers came. I looked for my salvation in the good which I tried to force on myself and my students. It was the time of good resolutions. It was also a time of total disaster, for I learned that it is truly the road to hell that is paved with good intentions.

My dear school now became hell to me, for everything about it ran against my striving. I suddenly felt alienated there. Earlier I had looked in the school for the light after the darkness that had frightened me on evil ways. Now I expected the school to be my fruitful field, but it bore only thorns and thistles. Of course, they had been there earlier as well, but I had paid them no attention, choosing to rejoice in the light that lay over them. In actual fact [31] I had earlier also regarded the school as my comforter, which was there, in a sense, for my benefit. That had not materially changed now, except that I did not now simply enjoy what was offered; I was determined to create in it what was destined to satisfy me. Still I felt that the school was there for my sake. That it would not give me what I believed I had a right to expect, despite my efforts, authority, and my presumed rights to the school; that is what turned it into my hell.

Now the rod was used to govern as never before. It became the means to coerce obedience and to teach me that such coerced obedience could never produce any good or create peace. In difficult hours of troublesome struggles I learned that a crushed opponent can never be a vanquished opponent. All that is needed is an opportunity for him to get his fingers free and avenge himself. Light and love vanished more and more from my school and gave way to the quiet before the storm.

But I had to have light so as not to become the prey of depravity and desolation. The light was there and it came when I needed it. Even now I cannot understand how my true friends never tired of me, and were always there with love and a kind of empathy whenever I found myself in extremity. Then, already, I marvelled at them, for I knew well that I had done nothing to merit their love. That had been amply proved by the departure of some so-called friends, which I fully deserved. These, however, stuck with me as I walked along the precipice of despair in the deepest darkness.

I was still capable in this time, however, of asking for the hand of one of the girls of Gnadenfeld to whom, in that one glorious year of my youth, I owed so much. She became my partner for life. With her came a veritable stream of light and clarity into my life at Pastwa. But it was also as the Gospel says: "The darkness has not comprehended the light." It did not comprehend this light either, and my Lene was at my side, but also a stranger, in the midst of the life in Pastwa. She cried often in those years.

That was now a new burden on my soul. I had now drawn a second innocent person into the circle of my wretched life and could do nothing to help ease it for her.

Now I collapsed totally. I had pursued my happiness in sin. But sin had betrayed me, made me its slave, saddled me with guilt, sucked out my life, and left me to despair. I had looked for liberation in politics but had found in it [32] nothing but malice and filth. Then I had turned to the good and found myself completely confounded because it was unattainable. And now my school had become estranged from me, and beside me a human being whom I loved with all my heart, lived wretchedly and did not know what had happened to her, nor why and for what purpose she had to suffer so. My duty towards this person, my wife, and the gift of our first little daughter, pulled me back from utter defeat. But I no longer had any idea where to turn to get help. Nothing was left now, except to grasp at the possibility of a miracle as the only way in which I could be rescued.

Not the world, nor what is in the world, indeed, not even the working of power that surrounds God, behind which I had not seen Him, and in spite of which I had finally even denied Him, no one and nothing else except God, "the God who does wonders," could save me.

* * * *

The time to which I have alluded now and again finally came in which I began to pray: "O God, if You are, reveal yourself to me and help me!" And God heard my prayer. The answer burst as light into one of the darkest moments of our life, in the hour of the death of our first little daughter. I have already recounted that. The experience wrought in me then led to the excitement of my first short story published in the *Friedensstimme*[3] with the title "Lord, Where Are You?" It is the last story in the little book *His Blood*. There I described what happened at that time, but I cannot explain it. It was exactly as the Apostle describes it in his letter to Titus:

> *For we ourselves were once foolish, disobedient, led astray, slaves to various passions and pleasures, passing our days in malice and envy, hated by others and hating one another; But when the goodness and loving kindness of God our Saviour appeared, He saved us, not because of deeds done by us in righteousness, but in virtue of His own mercy, by the washing of regeneration and renewal in the Holy Spirit.*

Yes, the goodness and loving kindness of God appeared when we needed them so desperately. They were there and saved us and that was the miracle. We experienced its truth and reality as an undeniable fact, but we can never explain it. So it was.

[33] On the morning after the death of our daughter in which the friendliness and courtesy of God had been revealed, I could not conduct the school. After the most necessary things had been looked after, my wife and I drove to Gnadenfeld to my parents. It was a frosty October day. A light mist lay over the expanse of countryside. The road was good and it seemed that even the horses understood us, for they trotted ahead steadily without veering aside so that we could hold hands and surrender to our feelings.

We were mostly silent, but we understood one another, and everything was so different. On this day I had for the first time

---

[3] *Voice of Peace*, a Mennonite Brethren church paper which first appeared in 1903.

consciously prayed to the God in whom I firmly believed. I had experienced Him in a wonderful way in my heart as the One who can, even in death, bring peace by His presence, and into whose hands we can safely commit our beginning, our middle and our end. Sin and guilt were no more; all had faded away. My own efforts had come to an end. Listening to the footsteps of the Father had begun, and attention to the prompting of His fatherly eyes. The soul's emptiness had been filled, and life was worth living because in following Him it led to a glorious destination. He knew the way, even if we did not and could make no plans for it, and we felt the blessedness of the Coming One with such certainty that nothing could have robbed us of that faith.

When the first school day after the funeral came, the classroom was full of sunshine. It penetrated my innermost being and uncovered for me an understanding so obvious, but which I had not been able to grasp thus far; it was the understanding to which I owe so much happiness and cheer in my teaching that I shall not neglect to be grateful for it to the end of my days; it was an understanding so simple that I laughed when I thought why it had not been part of my consciousness as self-evident from the beginning. I understood that the school and the students were not there for my sake, but that I was there for the sake of the school and the children.

Indeed, it was so self-evident. The parents paid me to serve them by teaching their children, not so that I would have someone to give me the required obedience. It was not the school that had to be constituted as I wished it for my own satisfaction; I had to be what the school expected of me.

On that day I finally surrendered the idea of becoming a marine engineer, and fell in love with the school as it was and sought then to shape it as it ought to be. I did it for the sake of the children and not for my own gratification. Now my work of teaching and nurture had a clear goal. [34] And as I lost my life for Christ's sake, I found it. When I abandoned the striving for my own gratification, I found the deepest satisfaction, mostly where I had least expected it. Where before I had been angry over every failure and each disobedience of the children as injustice that was directed at me personally, I now took pleasure in every evidence of love I received, and at every step ahead as a gift of grace which came to me above the salary I had agreed upon with the community. My work became so lively and interesting that I could no longer understand why anyone would find teaching troublesome and dreary.

Now everything I had experienced appeared in a new light. Often, in my mind, I stood on a mountain height and observed with shuddering the deep path of suffering I had walked, burdened by sin and guilt. And then my heart overflowed with gratitude toward God my Saviour, whose friendliness and generosity appeared and made me whole. The more often I looked at the road by which I had come, the more I forgot to hate and despise people. No matter what feelings may assert themselves in me toward my fellow humans, I know that I may not despise anyone, for I never know whether that person has been as sinful and guilty as I have been.

These are not mere words. For if I knew about my neighbour's one hundred sins, I know for a fact that there are thousands of my own. As soon as the sliver in my brother's eye angers me, the beam in my own eye hurts so much that I no longer want to think of the brother until the Lord Jesus has relieved me of my pain. Once that beam is gone, I cannot hate or despise my brother for the sake of his sliver. I can only regret that he cannot find the way to the Father through Christ, for if Christ could deal with my beam, should he not be able to remove the sliver from the eye of the other? Why do not more people seek the God who does wonders? If they were to look for Him, they would find Him as I found Him. And they would be blessed.

Chapter 4

The Enchanted Zone of Love

I now looked forward into life with new vision, and life took a new direction. Once I had learned to desire what was now my duty, namely to be a teacher, I was given what is normally considered to be a step up the ladder. People began to notice my writing, and through it I was privileged to speak to many. I was surrounded by good and interesting people. I saw their spiritual life, and was stimulated to study [35] it. I was especially attracted to those who were unattractive, to examine that unattractiveness in order to find the person hidden beneath it, who was writhing in pain and suffering much more from these shortcomings than those who for those same shortcomings despised and rejected him. That produced a remarkable result: the faltering, disobedient students became my special favourites.

These people who were usually neglected, or perhaps even hated and despised, proved to be more grateful and loving in their response than I could ever have dreamt. If we would understand that, we would devote much more effort to the unattractive, and would therefore also discover what splendid people they really are. For a teacher it is especially important to give special attention to these unappealing students, for one easily tolerates the likeable, and those who learn easily will do their lessons by themselves. But if one succeeds in finding a way to the heart of those with difficult personalities, one has certainly also won the others. A method by which the slow learners profit will certainly also be successful with the others.

Teaching and learning delighted me more and more, and it was not long before I passed the examinations to be a private tutor set by the Board of the teaching district of Kharkov. I earned a Five which was equivalent to *summa cum laude* [with highest honours]. Proud as a peacock I returned from Kharkov, left the primary school and took on the position, the task, which I have until now regarded as my life's work, if indeed I can even speak of a life's work when I think about my life. I became teacher of religion and German language at the newly opened girls' school in Ohrloff. The goal of this school was not to produce bluestockings, but to provide a fairly rounded education for future German housewives and mothers. Its aim was not primarily to impart great stores of knowledge, but a profound education of the character and the heart whereby the hunger for understanding would be awakened and the tools for independent thinking and investigation provided. For in the short time that the schools have the children and the youth they cannot do more than give them the desire for completing their education and some equipment for doing it. Schools that profess as their goal to provide their students with nothing more than a given fixed programme of knowledge and skills, even if they meet those objectives, usually do it at the expense of the best that human beings have – their gracious humanity, whose value goes beyond measurable goals.

Wherever this condition exists in the public schools, individual personality disappears and statistics prevail. As a student in such a school, [36] I will not be interested in who my teacher is, but in what he knows and can do for me. As soon as he has done that I am no longer interested in him. Students in such schools discuss the subjects they are studying there, but never the teachers who could be guides to things not yet thought of. Schools like that are much more supportive of international communism than the decrees of the Russian communists, which impel one to total resistance. If Russian autocracy had not crushed the living individuality out of the Russian citizen, the communists of today would have had their proper reward long ago. They can thank the wonderful efforts of the erstwhile so-called Ministry of Popular Education for the fact that they have been able to violate a great people for so long without paying the penalty. Those among the people who saw more clearly used to refer to that ministry as the Ministry for Popular Stupification.

Schools must teach people to think and discover for themselves. They should never imagine that they have done their duty when they have offered secondary information. The first duty of the elementary schools and those at the next level is to stimulate the desire to learn. Certainly that should not be neglected in the higher schools either, but the more mature student of the university already has a goal upon arrival. That student is mature enough to use the school to achieve those goals and does so. But the child is "sent" to school and arrives there without any initiative of its own. It has to be led, and this leading is much more important than is generally assumed. I make the bold claim that the elementary school in most cases sets the direction for the child's life and gives it those ideals which will be pursued from then on.

That is why it is so important that the right person is engaged to teach. He is to be the embodied ideal of his students which will stimulate them to emulate him and to search for the hidden fountains where the teacher finds the strength for his being, becoming, and action. The teacher's worth is measured not by the amount the students are able to memorize and cram into their mental files, but by being to them a personal guide, by the strength of the faith he is able to instill in them, by the brightness of the ideal he holds before them, and by the degree to which the miracle he commends to them is visible in him. I have always regarded it as something of a sin, which my father helped me to commit, that I became a teacher at age sixteen. And the curse follows from the sin. However, it is certainly God's wonderful grace that I have not been cursed for that sin to this day, nor have I in any particular way seen [37] the curse from that sin manifest itself in my students. On the other hand, the miracle is perhaps not so incomprehensible. For in the eyes of my students I was always someone who was struggling and becoming. They observed it even if perhaps they did not understand it. And that may have been the means in God's hand to avert the curse which should have come but did not.

* * * *

Before my conversion my life had fluctuated between sin and love. I experienced the curse of the one and the blessing of the other. After my conversion my life moved totally into the enchanted zone of love. Sin was still around me, lurking and exploiting every unwatchful moment to bring me down.

My wife was especially skilled in making a home of our house. She had gained some friends in Pastwa but was always more or less a stranger there. That was largely due to the depressing experiences which she had had to endure there in the first years of our marriage. In Friedensdorf[1] things were to be quite different.

As a man with a new lease on life, I came to Friedensdorf into a situation of extreme contrasts: on the one hand a rigid churchly conservatism, and on the other an exaggerated, passionate pietisim. Changes would have to be made. The body was actually quite sound, but it needed life. It was in this village that I became sharply aware for the first time of the special characteristics of our people, and I learned to love them. To be sure, through my conversion from sin, I had also been separated from my people. Mennonite culture did not appear to me to be so much valuable in its own right, as that it was material for the creating and fulfilling work of God's Spirit. There were young people here from whom something glorious could grow, if only we went about it the right way. The youth, like youth everywhere, wanted to sing from the heart, with warm feeling and ringing voices. But churchly conservatism raised its head and cautioned, "Easy, easy! Our forefathers did not do that and we shouldn't either. Singing practice?! Our new teacher wants to start singing practice?!" Well, that would remain to be seen. Teacher So-and-So had once tried that and had sent a note around inviting the young people to a singing practice. But this note had fallen into the hands of the late *Ohm*[2] H., and he had torn it up without hesitation. This teacher [38] So-and-So (who still lives somewhere in this evil world and occasionally

---

[1] A village about 12 km northwest of Gnadenfeld.

[2] *Ohm* is the Low German word for *uncle*, and like the High German *Onkel*, was used by Mennonites as a term of respect for older men in the community.

authors something) wrote an essay for the *Odessaer Zeitung*[3] with the title *We and Abdera*[4] and thus scuttled the whole thing.

When I heard that story I reasoned that something similar could happen to me too if I was not careful. I conceived the cunning idea never to write a note and to make the whole thing as unofficial as possible, and then one day present the world of Friedensdorf with a *fait accompli*. No doubt about it, notes that are not written cannot be torn up. I knew an *Ohm* who was waiting for a note to destroy it. I was determined that he should have no chance at it.

My wife had already made friends with some of the young people. They came to visit and she sang to them beautifully accompanied on her guitar. Small wonder that the youngsters began to sing along. This happened by accident in our house, not in the schoolroom. When the weather was nice, we went out onto the open veranda. It was large, and equipped with the most comfortable garden furniture I ever knew. There we sat and played and sang without it being a formal singing practice. The determined-to-tear-the-note *Onkel* did not know how to respond. Singing together during a social gathering was not against the tradition. In his estimation it was certainly not proper for the undeniably truly married wife of the teacher to socialize with the young unmarrieds. That was certainly not the generally accepted practice. Alas, new things invaded even Friedensdorf and one could not do much about it except to sigh a little. The fact that the teacher gave his guests song sheets on which the music was written in numerical notation[5] certainly smelled suspiciously of singing practice, but even that could not be prevented. If only there had been a note! Then one could have destroyed it and that would have been that.

---

[3] The *Odessaer Zeitung* was a German language paper first published in Odessa in 1863.

[4] Abdera was a seaport of ancient Thrace whose inhabitants were proverbial for their stupidity. Abdera was also the birthplace of Democritus, the laughing philosopher. Presumably teacher So-and-So thought of himself as the philosopher laughing at the stupidity of Friedensdorf.

[5] The numerical system of music notation called *Ziffern* (numbers), was much used by Mennonites in Russia. It was developed in France in the 17th century.

One evening this *Onkel* stood on the side of the street across from where we were singing and making music on the veranda. He wanted to form a judgment about the matter. As my neighbour T. later told me, the old man had expressed his judgment as he walked away. What he said was, "Wow, do they ever sing beautifully. The teacher's wife has a good voice, and Bergen's Barbie can be heard a long way off."

The group of singers grew ever larger. One evening money was collected to get a hectograph[6] and a large bright lamp. I looked after both. The next, and official, singing practice was scheduled for the coming Thursday evening. And it took place as planned, and in the schoolroom, since our residence could no longer contain all the singers. [39]

Now the hour had come when the *Onkel* believed he must intervene, for this was a full-blown, undisguised singing practice. Resolutely, he stepped into the brightly lit schoolroom as we sang *Hand in hand with Jesus I will safely go*. He stood by the door, waiting until we were finished. When we stopped, he evidently thought that he might as well listen to the next song as well. We sang *Wie bist du mir so innig gut, mein Hoher Priester Du* [How well you love me, my High Priest]. When the song was over the *Onkel* could not say anything because a tenacious, thick lump had lodged in his throat. He could not really come forward either because there was a treasonable glint in his eye which he did not want us to see. So we sang again with happy hearts: *Freuet euch des Herrn! Ja freuet euch ihr Gerechten! Preisen sollen ihn die Frommen!* [Rejoice in the Lord! Rejoice you righteous ones! Praise him all you who are just!] When the aria was done the *Onkel* quietly went out the door. When next Thursday came, all three of his daughters also came to practice. The good cause had triumphed once again. To achieve the victory, my wife had provided the positive: she had begun to sing. I supplied the negative: I wrote no note. But it was the goodness of the issue itself that finally overcame all opposition.

* * * *

---

[6] A chemical duplicating process, forerunner of the photocopier.

It appeared to me, however, that the other matter which I thought necessary, the organization of a Bible study, would be more difficult.

Oddly enough, I was convinced that it could not be done without a note. There was a Bible study in the village, but its reputation was such that even members of the Mennonite Brethren who had moved into the village could not support it, not to mention the Church Mennonites,[7] for whom a Bible study was diametrically against all tradition.

As for me, I had an urgent desire to share of myself and to learn from the spiritual experiences of others. I longed to discover the treasures of the precious Word of God in a common search. I yearned for the close fellowship of the Word in the Spirit. I knew that there was far more depth in much that was discussed in village meetings than a superficial observer could sense. However, I felt that what was in those depths, and what made the heart so joyful, should be free to flow out clearly and without any hindrance from hearts God had blessed with His grace. I fervently wanted a Bible study. I had to have a Bible study. I spoke to my wife about it. She agreed with me, but added that she could not help me with this as she had helped me with the singing. [40] There was nothing for it; we had to wait until God in His wonderful way once again quite obviously intervened to help.

There is a long story connected to this that goes back to the time before I was born, when my father was teacher in Steinbach.[8] One day he sat in front of the door of the Steinbach school in the deepening twilight of the evening. Suddenly he heard two voices in violent argument, interspersed by the rattle of wagon wheels and the sound of horses, down by the bridge. "I will drive!" "No, you won't!" As my father walked towards them, he saw that a strong youth was holding the horses by the bridle and pushing them back while the man who sat on the wagon tried to get them to go in the direction of the tavern up on the hill. "I will drive!" "No, you won't!" When the two noticed my father nearby, they stopped

---

[7] The term *Kirchliche* (churchly) was used to distinguish the traditional Mennonites from the Mennonite Brethren.

[8] A small village about 10 km southwest of Gnadenfeld.

their argument. The younger let go of the horses' bridles and stepped towards the wagon. The older allowed him to get in. And off they went, not to the tavern, but northwards out of the estate. Here, too, the good had triumphed. The one who had barred the way to the tavern was Peter, the son of the old man Bondar-Sperling from Waldheim.[9] This man had resisted sin in the power of God who does wonders even when it attacked him with great power. He had gone the way of salvation. When I was teacher in Friedensdorf, he was already a man of advanced age. He had a big family which he managed to hold together in a remarkable way. He was quite well-to-do, a fact which his village contemporaries could not grasp.

One of the inconsiderate among us – and some of them can be quite disgracefully inconsiderate – one day drove onto the Sperlings' yard. Sperling had bought the best farm in the village, next to the school, complete with all the equipment, had moved in, and was just then getting everything into place. He was a member of the Mennonite Brethren Church. This inconsiderate person came racing onto the Sperling yard in a light carriage, his horses at a gallop, making a neat circle in front of the big granary that lay at right angles to house and barn, and coming to an abrupt stop in front of the veranda on which the unassuming *Ohm* Sperling stood.

"Good day! Are you a Sperling?"

"Yep, that's who I am, and furthermore only one of the ordinary grey kind."[10]

"Where did you get all of this?" asked the inconsiderate neighbour. [41]

"From my Father," came the answer.

"Indeed, and who was your father? Aren't you one of the Waldheim Bondar-Sperlings?"

"True, that's where I come from."

"Don't talk foolishness then. From whom did you get all this?"

"From my Father," came the patient reply.

"That's totally impossible."

---

[9] A village about 8 km northwest of Gnadenfeld.

[10] *Sperling* is German for "sparrow."

"It is certainly possible," replied *Ohm* Sperling. "Indeed, my Father has much more than that. He just does not see fit to give it to me as yet." At that point the churl realized whom Sperling was talking about.

"Oh, so that's what you mean. Well, good-bye."

And with that the fine carriage rattled out of the gate.

Another time a Russian came onto the yard. The Russians could not believe that everything was above board with all that German wealth. They were certain that some secret chicanery must be involved.

"Where is your money machine?" asked the Russian half in jest, half with bitter envy.

"Come on, I'll show it to you," replied *Ohm* Sperling, and led the astonished man into a shed where the farm implements were stored. He showed his visitor a new plough which he had just acquired.

"That," he said, "is my money machine."

After one thing and another had been said, the discussion turned to the belief that God has to give His blessing to a person's work if it is to succeed. *Ohm* Sperling helped the Russian to get a proper plough, and through all the years the two remained good friends. The Russian also learned to make money with the German machine, and also found Him who gives growth to the seed we sow.

This *Ohm* Sperling God now gave me for a neighbour. He, too, was not happy with the existing Bible study in Friedensdorf and longed for another. I talked to him about my concern, and very quickly he gave me simple, practical advice that could easily be put into practice. On the evening of the same day Sperling, followed by his prematurely aged wife, came to our place through the garden. Under his arm he carried his Bible, according to the inviolable Mennonite custom. There was something ceremonial about this coming and I noticed that something special was in the making.

"We are having a Bible study at your house tonight," said *Ohm* Sperling after the two had sat down.

"Yes, well, that is, how . . .?"

"You do have a Bible and a hymn book, don't you? Get them! [42] We'll sing a song, you pray with us, and we study a portion of Scripture, and that will be our Bible study."

It was much too simple. I had not even written a note. But I went and got Bible and hymn book. My wife sat down with us. We sang *O, wie freu'n wir uns der Stunde* [How joyful for us is the hour]. The sound was a bit thin, but beautiful nevertheless. Then we read I John 1 and discussed it. In closing we knelt down and prayed together.

"Next Friday the Bible study is at our place," said *Ohm* Sperling as they left. And that is what happened.

The time after that, we met again at our house and a few people from the village joined us. A few more meetings like that, and the room was full, and the Lord was with us and blessed us. That is how we began a Bible study in Friedensdorf, and if I am not mistaken, it continues there to this day.

I stayed in Friedensdorf only two years and they were good years. In Rosenort,[11] to which we moved next, I worked for three years. In the year 1906 I was chosen as minister of the Gnadenfeld congregation and on November 19th of that year ordained into the ministry by the old revered elder Heinrich Dirks. After that, there was much work to do. Two years later in 1908, as I already mentioned, I wrote and passed my examination in German [language and literature] and took a position at the Ohrloff[12] Girls' School. I remained there until the Bolsheviks rather ungently removed me from that position.

* * * *

Those years were filled with work. The school demanded all my time for much was planned that had to be accomplished. The principal of the school was, for good or ill, a very enterprising woman, and seemed to be made for the work she had to do. She was a girl with the girls and at the same time guide, teacher and mother to them.

Our objective was to win the girls for their studies as well as for a serious but happy way of life, and to provide them with as much as

---

[11] A village about 28 km southwest of Gnadenfeld.

[12] Ohrloff lay a few km southwest of Rosenort.

possible for the road. That had been the intention of the association at the founding of the school. Since true cheerfulness and serious thoughtfulness can grow and persist only in the soil of Christian faith, care had been taken that thorough instruction in religion should be part of the programme. Those hours of religious studies were always times of blessing.

Considerable space had also been given in the curriculum to Russian and German literature. Although our wise government had in those days decreed that "The German language must be instructed in the Russian language,"[13] we still managed [43] thoroughly to enjoy the treasures of German literature.

The study of literature, however, naturally demanded literary soirées.[14] This was the plain on which the battle was joined. We had only girls in the school, but all the classical plays had failed to consider this problem and had always included male roles. In the Catholic *Mädchenbühne*[15] we found much that was good but rarely anything classical. Most of it was somewhat sentimental and we could not use much of it. On top of that, these things, part and parcel, were more or less unfamiliar to our culture. We had to spend a lot of time explaining it all to the girls and then also to our esteemed public.

All my fingers began to tingle and I could not resist the urge: I wrote *De Bildung*,[16] rehearsed it with my girls, and presented it at one of the literary evenings as an addition to the programme. I received the world's "gratitude" for it. Nevertheless, I was urged to publish it, which I did, and for which I also got it in the neck. The thing caused me considerable suffering. Be that as it may, *De Bildung* continues to speak to our people

---

[13] The emergence of Russian nationalism in the late nineteenth century directly affected Mennonites, as all communication with Imperial officials had to be in Russian after 1870. Though anti-German and anti-Mennonite sentiments were first voiced at that time, the rhetoric worsened steadily as relations between Germany and the Russian empire deteriorated after 1890.

[14] *Literaturabende* or "literaries" as they were called among Mennonites in Canada until the 1950s.

[15] "The Girls' Stage," probably a school magazine.

[16] Low German for "education."

to this day. Less controversial was *Daut Schultebott*,[17] which I wrote for the students at the secondary school, but then it was also worth less. Dead silence greeted *De Enbildung*,[18] and rightly so. The last two pieces belong to the past. May their ashes rest in peace! Perhaps they were never anything but dust and ashes.

The immediate consequence of the writing and play acting was that together we began to notice that literature could occasionally touch us in a very personal and sensitive way. That meant paying much closer attention to it; the literary evenings occurred more frequently and people preferred those which dealt with Mennonite themes. Thus, a lively custom of singing and reciting began among the Mennonite folk in South Russia. This is not to say that *De Bildung* had called Mennonite literature into being. Such literature was already there. But perhaps it did receive a little nudge from this much-decried play.

Gradually the number of literary evenings increased in number and in quality in all our schools. And when we had finally come so far that our hearts were no longer filled with horror when we had boys and girls together in the same room under our supervision, we even put on a lengthy excerpt from Glinka's opera *A Life for the Czar*. The singing that evening could have been a lot worse.

One of the great advantages of the literary evenings for our work was that they made it possible to present clearly and compare carefully the treasures of literature, both our own [44] as well as those from outside. It sharpened our judgment and provided a way for our students but also for the broader masses of our people to choose the good from the vast quantity of literary products and to reject the inferior.

The following is a good example of what could happen. There was a group of girls whom we had been unable to persuade concerning the goals and purposes of our school. They regarded the school as an institution of torture in which their parents kept them imprisoned. We

---

[17] Meeting of the village council.
[18] Conceit.

teachers were the spoilsports who commanded what was unbearable and forbade what was enjoyable. These girls requested the permission to present at the next literary evening a silly skit, which they considered to be incredibly funny. As a matter of principle we allowed the students to choose what was to be presented. That compelled them to careful consideration. Our hall was always crowded on those evenings, and whoever had chosen or presented something was exposed to the criticism of the crowd. So care was the watchword, for they were concerned for approval and did not want to be disgraced before all the guests.

I knew immediately that these naughty girls had chosen that piece in a mood of rebellion, and they stuck to their determination despite our warnings. And even if I had not surmised this, they did not hide their feelings. "You never allow us to do anything jolly," said the girl who spoke for the group, her lips pouting. "We are still young and you want us to act like old people who no longer like to laugh." A deep sigh could be heard from her cohorts and the whisper, "They spoil all our fun." "You will present your piece," I decided then and there, and my colleagues stared at me, speechless.

The girls hesitated before they left. They sensed something sinister behind this permission. Finally they went, but evidently not especially pleased with the permission they had been given. When they had gone, Miss Willms said: "Whatever are you thinking, Mr. Janzen? All of us will be disgraced if that stupid thing is presented." "Let me take care of it," I said. There was some shaking of heads, but they did not interfere with me or the girls.

Many of our more pious folk, some of them converted and some not, could never quite understand my labours towards the understanding of literature. Occasionally I was asked whether I could also pray for the success of a literary evening. [45] And how I prayed! How I felt the weight of the responsibility with which I worked! Certainly I prayed fervently for the coming evening, for I had started down a very unusual road. It was risky to put on a bad piece in order that good might come of it.

My prayers were heard. One day during the preparations, the girls came to me and asked when I would rehearse the piece with them. I had expected this, but looked at them with astonishment. "I have not prevented you from choosing something you like," I said. "You may do that which will please you. But you cannot seriously expect me to rehearse a piece with you that I don't approve of since I think it's foolish. Obviously you think differently. So, prove to me that you are right in this. You will need to decide how you do it. I would only spoil the piece for you if I were to meddle with it, since I think it's no good, and also believe that you can't do anything with it." Dejected, they left, and I thought they would abandon their plan. But I was mistaken. Through their folly they were driven deeper and deeper into their own mischief, just as had once happened to me. I noticed that they went to work and practiced to spite us. I was also aware that their enthusiasm for the whole thing began to diminish more and more.

When the programme was planned, they allowed their piece to be included. It was named, the names of the producers listed, and the actresses identified. The programme was duplicated on the hectograph, and after some hundreds of copies had been made, the girls wanted their play taken off. Now I objected. Once the piece was on the programme, how could it be replaced, since tomorrow was the day?

The programme had been prepared with special care by the teachers and the responsible girls with the expressed intention of letting the foolish choice of the rebels stand out in plain view. Our plan succeeded beyond expectation. The girls could hardly complete their offering. The longer it went on, the more clearly they saw how they were disgracing themselves. Beside all the good that had already been offered, the banal mediocrity of their play was so distasteful that they had to notice and understand. After the curtain came down, loud crying could be heard. Generous [46] promises were made that such a thing would never happen again.

Now what? I asked our little sinners, who had now become penitents, whether they expected me to assume the responsibility before our audience for what they had presented. Remorseful as they were, they could not now expect this of me, but neither did they want to step out and explain it themselves. They begged me to do it. The pause was now becoming quite long, and it was high time to give the audience the explanation that was owed. While preparations were made behind the curtain for the next presentation, I stepped out and gave a short talk on the problems of teaching literature and the difficulty in solving them. The matter was dealt with. I would not advise anyone to repeat that stratagem. We were skirting very close to the edge, but in the end, what we had anticipated and prayed for was accomplished.

We never had a repetition of that. We were able to distribute the materials for the literary events among our students without worrying. They were very careful that they did not shoot themselves in the foot and came to us for advice on difficult problems. Once questions are asked, it is easy to teach.

The cultivation of the good and the beautiful was a great pleasure for us. The girls gladly came to singing practice at 7:30 a.m. every day. We preferred to sing six times a week in the morning with renewed energy rather than twice a week in the afternoon when we were tired, and when the air in the classroom was no longer pure. And how we sang! When I speak about that in our house now, our satirist, sniffing loudly, asks, "Would someone please open a window?" as much as to say: self-praise smells. I will not argue that this could not be the case, but I can only say: We sang very well. In 1913, at the Green Limetree in Greifswald [Germany] a small group of German teachers struggled to learn a couple of German folk songs. I will say no more except that on that occasion I should like to have had my "Russian lasses" there to show those German school teachers what a German folk song is! Yes, indeed! I know that self-praise smells. Open doors and windows when you read this, but we sang well! Indeed!

Life went on around our school, and public opinion expressed itself for or against our work and our methods. I do not know whether removing me from the school for my heresies ever came up for discussion. The [47] pious people, converted and unconverted, denied me the pulpit for a time, the former because my actions really seemed questionable to them, the others because they could not miss any opportunity to show me what their principles were. I felt sorry for the former and I carefully weighed their criticisms. I genuinely tried to ascertain whether I could honestly see something I had done wrong, to repent for it, and promise not to do it again. When in my judgment I found such a case, I apologized through the *Friedensstimme* [Voice of Peace]. But once I had the printed notice before me, I felt it was not quite truthful. I could not regret what, after careful consideration I had done, knowing all the time that I did it with the intention of serving the Lord and my people. I was not insulted that they forbade me the pulpit. They had to do it. Those who were honest felt compelled in their consciences to do it. And those who were not honest? I felt sorrier for them than for the others. They were the truly unfortunate ones in the whole matter.

Without bitterness I sat as often as I could below the pulpit from which I was not allowed to speak. I accepted whatever came to me and as much as my heart was able to receive. And the solemn day came when I was again allowed to preach, and many a time I witnessed from that place for my Lord and Master before I emigrated to Canada.

However, while I was forbidden to preach at home, I was often asked to serve with the Word elsewhere. Along with my teaching, I assumed responsibility for the care of the small city church in Melitopol. I served that congregation, with some interruptions, until the Bolsheviks put an end to it.

Chapter 5

The Altonau Poplars

War broke out, and in 1915 I had to enter the service. I was drafted in September and found myself first on the Alt Berdjaner *Forstei*.[1] Under very easy-going superiors, I went through all the stages from picking rosehips to sweeping rooms to hauling water. It was a curious sensation to be cutting trees near the highway and see people driving freely on that road who could go where they wished. My steps were all prescribed for me. I was not far from home, only eighteen verst, that is twelve miles [19 km].

I now became acquainted with the *Forstei* as a man. It had once helped raise me as a child. It was not the same in name and place, but identical in its character. [48] If you drove beyond the last Mennonite village, Altonau, in the direction of the *Forstei*, the road took you over a small dam on each side of which stood very tall poplars. Those who served on the *Forstei* said that one had to hang one's conscience on these poplars and pick it up again on the return journey, for inside there was no

---

[1] This forestry camp was located not far from the southwest end of the Molotschna Colony.

need for it. Of course this was meant facetiously, but it was in fact difficult to be conscientious on the *Forstei*.

For one thing, the workers on the *Forstei* could not find any purpose in the work they did, therefore had no interest in it, and also no sense of satisfaction. If now we consider that to the impure all things are impure, it becomes quite clear that this work, pointless in and of itself, did indeed save us from having to bear arms, but that, as an unjustified *Privilegium*[2] (privilege) guaranteed by the Emperor, it had a deteriorating effect upon our youth. The unconverted conscript, although born in the protection of the Mennonite community, was no Christian and therefore also not a Mennonite, for he could not accept or reject the exemption on the grounds of conscience. There could be other reasons for him to make choices for or against this or that, perhaps even for or against bearing arms, but that gave him no right to the enjoyment of a privilege, which had once been granted by the government to protect faith and Christian conviction. Most of the young men were received as members of the church before they were drafted. But they were by no means all convinced Christians nor convinced weaponless Mennonites who performed a useless service honestly and in the obedience of faith, and who therefore even in this service, took "pains to have a clear conscience toward God and toward man" [Acts 24:16]. Anyone who knows the *Forstei* camps will make no attempt to argue that they had an ennobling effect on our people or our Christian faith.

It is worth considering to what extent the *Forstei* service nurtured the widespread view among our people that one should never sell a bad cow for a high price within the circumference of the Mennonite colonies, but that one could certainly do so beyond the Altonau poplars.

Now, if our loving God still does not allow dense concentrations of Mennonites in Canada, perhaps that is because He wishes to teach us that

---

[2] Mennonites who arrived in the Russian empire before 1800 first negotiated a *Privilegium* or charter of privileges that included everything from the promise of permanent exemption from military service and freedom of religion, to financial subsidies and tax exemptions. Though promised as a formal document in 1787, Mennonites had to wait until Tsar Paul I officially granted them this charter in 1800.

non-Mennonites also have human rights.[3] If we regard the refusal to swear the oath as one of our identifying characteristics, whose spiritual foundation must be absolute truthfulness insofar as we know it, then we must deal honestly with all people, if we are not to become hypocrites.

Certainly believers had ample opportunity to confess their Lord courageously in the *Forstei*. But for this reason they were occasionally [49] so provoked that one could justifiably call what happened to them persecution. Sometimes this persecution by Mennonites against Mennonites approached violence. While such cases were rare, those who took the principles of their faith seriously were frequently subject to mockery and contempt. It was not easy for them to endure this day after day without becoming tired and discouraged.

My father praised the *Forstei* service for teaching the youth discipline and order. He approached the training of the service men with the zeal and understanding and love for them which were his trademark. However, should his memoirs ever become public, they will reveal how he suffered under the hopelessness of the effort, how the bitter struggle broke him, and how his one joy was that through his efforts a few could be rescued from destruction. His positive efforts were often opposed in a cunning manner, sometimes by trickery and sometimes also with rude tactlessness, organized and led by the *starshii* [foreman] of the command. Sometimes, on the other hand, these leaders in the command were earnest Christians of good will, ready to support the good for which he stood. A few of these are still alive today. I take this occasion to call out to them in the name of my late father, "God reward you!"

The reader will already have concluded that, although I grew up in the *Forstei*, and served there as a man, I never became a friend of the *Forstei* and its service. Nor am I a friend of privileges, for I consider them

---

[3] Mennonites had initially been granted vast tracts of land for settlement in the Russian empire for which they were entirely responsible. They quickly became both "church" and "state," mayors as well as ministers, at least at the local level. By contrast, Mennonites who came to Canada in the 1920s settled in individual towns – as opposed to block settlements – and within existing municipalities; hence the difference in "concentration" described here.

to be unjust even if they were conferred by the highest authority, and even if we possess and enjoy these privileges which others do not have.

It was unjust when they tried to coerce us into military service against our convictions. Because of our faith, we had moral and juridical claims to alternative, noncombatant service, provided that we were personally convinced of being nonresistant and not merely protesting a war. However, this alternative service should in no way be easier or less dangerous than the military service rendered by non-Mennonite citizens of the state. For citizens of the same state should also have the same obligations and rights. As long as a state is governed by Christian principles, it will respect the consciences of its citizens and take the distinctive features of their faith into consideration so that their citizenship may never cause them to betray their beliefs. But that state will not give any group of its citizens a specific privilege and expect the rest to carry the burdens. A just state seeks to take individual characteristics into account, but distributes the obligations equally on all shoulders.

To the argument that we paid for our *Privilegium* in Russia [50] by paying much higher taxes than other citizens of the country, I say: I would not surrender my son for all the taxes ever paid in Russia. The Russian "baba" who gave up her son in mistaken but nevertheless faithful love for the Fatherland, made a sacrifice to the state a thousand times greater than all the nonresistant Mennonites with all their taxes. True, many a Mennonite has given his life for his homeland in noncombatant service in the last war [WW I], and the Russians cannot accuse us. I speak against the *Privilegium*. Never again should we seek to gain one. Let us render noncombatant service, but a service that is in no sense easier or less dangerous than service with weapons. Anyone who is concerned to know what such a service might be, should come to me. Believe me, I know. I know of one which would be of incalculable value to the state, much to our own good and promote the honour of our Lord Jesus Christ. This service would be no easier and no safer than military service. When on one occasion I suggested this service in Russia, the response was: why should we take on any burdens which are not forced on us? So far I have not found anything in Scripture that says that we should strive for righteousness only when we are coerced to it. On the contrary, I believe that if we reject something that is unjust even though it is of external advantage to us, we will not be acting against our conscience.

I certainly have no desire to reproach our fathers who, in the past, agreed to accept the forestry service. Nor do I accuse our ancestors for accepting the *Privilegium* when first they came to Russia. Those, however, who did not take preventive action when they could see corruption coming, they bear the guilt for our spiritual impoverishment. Those bear the guilt who want only praise and cannot abide any criticism; they reject it only because it is not cheap flattery. Those bear the guilt who are convinced that humanity consists of Mennonites and a negligible remnant of those who believe otherwise. Those bear the guilt, be they from the *Kirchengemeinde*, the Mennonite Brethren, or the Alliance,[4] who have the appearance of godliness in adult baptism, baptism by sprinkling, baptism by immersion, open communion, closed communion, the confession of nonresistance, refusal of the oath and other similar convictions, but deny the power of them. Those bear the guilt who always back away from an open and honest confession of sin, because confession includes the pledge to forsake sin.

In the year 1905 we should have paid attention, should have critically examined our stance on nonresistance, and foreseen the consequences.[5] I will never forget the moment on the grounds of the mayoral office of Friedensdorf when I pressed a Russian New Testament into the hands of a reserve soldier [51] who was leaving for the war against Japan. He was the same age as I, and had I not been a Mennonite, I would have had to go as well. As it was, my life did not change a whit while others were dying. I do not deny that the occasion of the war was folly and that all the bloodletting brought no blessing, especially not for

---

[4] The Alliance churches were two congregations that did not belong to either the *Kirchliche* or the Mennonite Brethren. See *The Mennonite Encyclopedia*, vol. I, p. 62.

[5] The Russian empire experienced a terrible crisis after 1904, as the empire became embroiled in a war with Japan. Despite expectations of an easy victory, Russians were quickly in retreat, and eventually compelled to surrender vast tracts in Manchuria. The war effort contributed to the revolt of 1905, which threatened the end of the monarchy itself before order was restored in the late fall of that year. This pattern of a dismal war effort leading to a revolt was repeated a decade later, with fatal consequences for the Romanov monarchy.

Russia. But those people believed they were obligated to their homeland even to dying for it. We paid for our *Privilegium* by generously supporting the families of the recruited reservists from the nearby Russian villages, but never ate even one piece of bread and butter less during that whole difficult time. A great number of citizens offered everything, even their very life, while we supported them from our surplus.

A few of our young men felt the whole thing illogical, and volunteered for the medical corps, and exposed themselves to the dangers of war without bearing weapons. They did not inflict wounds, but bound up wounds at peril to their lives. Most, however, continued to serve in the *Forstei*.

However, I have wandered away from my original topic. The forestry service with everything that came in its wake is in my judgment a dark chapter of our history. When the World War [WW I] broke out, we no longer knew where we stood.[6] The serious situation into which we were suddenly placed forced us to reflection. The message that came from our pulpits, hesitantly at the beginning, was that our young men should volunteer for the medical corps, and that many did so became for us a great blessing. In the trouble and danger of that service, one's personal worth emerged. Here also it was possible to live one's faith. Our medical corpsmen soon earned the favour of their superiors, and what was even more important, the favour, the appreciation, and the love of the sick and wounded Russian soldiers for whom they cared.

But what about all the rest of us? All of the Mennonite congregations together did not have the means to provide chaplains for the ranks of the medical personnel. They were allowed to do it at their own expense, but they did not do it. The medical corpsmen in the Caucasus especially complained of this neglect.

---

[6] The First World War presented a serious challenge to Mennonites: How could they demonstrate their loyalty to the Russian empire and still be truthful to their pacifist religion? At the same time, anti-German hysteria resulted in severe restrictions on all things German, and culminated in the so-called "Liquidation Laws" of 1915-1917, which made possible the seizure of German-owned estates along the western frontier.

But when the statute of expropriation hovered over us and was carried out to a degree, we had hundreds of thousands with which to bribe high officials to suspend that law. Unfortunately, the ministers were reluctant to receive these "gifts," and that was our greatest concern. How happy we were when we finally learned that Minister Dobrovolsky would graciously accept our hundred thousands. Whether that was really true, one does not know, but that is what we heard and we breathed easier. "Alas," that government was then so near its end that we never had the opportunity to [52] experience Dobrovolsky's generosity.

We had no money to send out chaplains, for that concerned only human souls, the immortal souls of our sons and brothers. But we did have money to bribe the officials, for there the concern was land, that is, the foundations of our existence and culture. God be merciful to us sinners! And if the elders did it, what could be expected from the young?

There were those who felt the imbalance instinctively. They were like the many who in 1874 and 1875 emigrated to America because of an instinctive anxiety about the new *Privilegium*.[7] They chose the heavy burden of a dangerous pioneer life rather than to remain in the warm nest and enjoy that questionable *Privilegium*.

During the World War many responded similarly, especially the young who were in the *Forstei*. So they volunteered for the medical corps, and some also for active military service. But they were rejected by the government because they were German. That was a very sobering experience. In the year 1917 a large number of young men met in a congress in Halbstadt against the will of their elders. There they adopted the wonderful, unanimous resolution in which they confessed their commitment to nonresistance. In their fiery enthusiasm for the new order that was coming, they knew that their commitment to their rejection of

---

[7] Approximately a third of Mennonites in Imperial Russia migrated to North America in 1874, in part because of the threatened elimination of their permanent exemption from military service, as well as the promise of better economic opportunities in Manitoba and Kansas.

the sword was total. But when the new order turned out to be so different than we all expected, the *Selbstschutz*[8] was organized in 1918 despite that wonderful resolution. The *Selbstschutz* led directly to regular military service.

What an array of contradictions pressed together in so short a space of time! We no longer knew where we stood. The high poplars of Altonau broke down, likely under the burden of the many Mennonite consciences that had been hung on them and were perhaps forgotten there.

During the preceding years the Mennonites had allowed themselves to be surrounded by a number of forms and usages. They had all done it, the *Kirchliche*, the Brethren, and the Alliance. The difference between them was that with the latter, the forms were still a bit newer, shinier. But they were forms nevertheless, empty, if they did not contain anything. Whatever was included in these forms was Mennonite, and therefore good. Whatever questioned those forms or whatever stood outside, was non-Mennonite, and therefore also of less value or even bad.

When the wind of tribulation roared through our ranks, all that [53] was empty began to sway dangerously, and some of it simply collapsed.[9] Later, however, when the storm had abated somewhat, it was all built up again, so that now we stand again as Mennonites without fear and blemish. For the salvation of our people whom I love with all my soul, I could desire for them a little more fear and also some more blemishes. In Canada we stand at the beginning of a new era of our history. If only we could avoid the mistakes which were made in the period through which we just passed! There, now I've said it. My people, you may despise and reject me, but turn from your sins, so that the Lord may raise you up again. It is for that reason that I have written all these bitter words.

---

[8] Literally "self-defence," or "self-protection." The term refers to a fighting force of Mennonites organized to protect the Mennonite colonies against the anarchists led by Nestor Makhno. In the Molotschna it reached a fighting force of 2,700. The picture of a purely defensive force presented here is challenged by others who paint a more aggressive picture of it. By that interpretation, the *Selbstschutz* involved the less-than-pious sons of Mennonite estate owners whose actions were at times foolishly aggressive.

[9] Reference is to the tumultuous years of world war, revolution, and civil war, 1914-1921.

And you Americans,[10] don't waste your time by sitting in judgment on us. That will bring you small blessing. Rather, let our profoundly sad story be a warning to you. Discern your weakness, seek to know the reasons for them, and let Christ remove them, so that you do not experience a worse fate.

* * * *

In hard times I learned that individuals among us achieve much more than the organized whole. Quite recently someone said to me: "Sure, your school was operated by an association. It's easy for you to talk. Our school was a regional school which could not count on nearly so much interest. For us it was much more difficult." But school associations were composed of individual persons who had an interest in the matter. The regional schools, on the other hand, were supported by all the people living in the region. The individuals with their commitment moved history forward. The mass of people could never accomplish very much.

The reason for that is perhaps that in our churches the right of self-determination was held in such high regard. It provided the possibility for the individual to achieve something independent of the majority. The whole community with its particular structure provided the soil out of which the individual grew, and in which he lived and developed. Thank God, there always were individuals who were concerned, so that what was most necessary did in the end get done. The leaders of our community in that time had my sympathy. They were no longer helmsmen and engineers who kept our little Mennonite ship going at full steam towards a better future. They could only try to slow it down so that it would not drift into the whirlpool too quickly and founder there. They have been poorly rewarded for that service. It is a thankless task to have to slow down a wagon that is plummeting down a mountainside [54] rather than to take it up the trail.

I spoke earlier with strong enthusiasm about our schools. That could create the impression that I did it because I was a teacher in Russia

---

[10] He seems to mean all North American Mennonites who did not share the bitter experiences in Russia.

myself. My judgment may indeed be somewhat coloured by this fact, but in the time of tribulation something happened that greatly strengthened my enthusiasm for teachers and schools.

Before the war there had always been a more or less good-natured antagonism between teachers and farmers. It had the one negative effect that teachers had no voice in community affairs. Occasionally there were also complaints when, now and then, teachers were elected to a responsible position. When the hard times came and leaders were needed, it happened that almost everywhere, teachers were elected to leadership. They were, after all, members of farming families and closely linked to agriculture, and so the antagonism referred to could not be taken seriously. By accident or otherwise, a teacher was elected to head the agricultural society. The vice-chairman was also a teacher. Virtually all the church elders in the Molotschna were teachers. The secretary of the Commission for Church Affairs was a teacher, and in the year 1924 all three Commission members were teachers. There was a tendency to dissatisfaction in some places because these impractical teachers, who before the war did not even have the vote, were now everywhere in leadership positions. But there seemed to be no alternative. It therefore became the thankless task of the teachers to apply the brakes to that wagon plunging down the mountain to whatever degree was possible.

It is said that the German school teachers won the Franco-Prussian War. Why should not the Mennonite teachers of South Russia be given the honour that, in very difficult times, they stepped into the breach for the welfare of their people and prevented a catastrophe? Enough said: what the *Forstei* destroyed, the schools were able in part to restore again. If it were ever necessary for the *Forstei* service to be repeated, I should vigorously oppose it. To the same degree I long for a restoration of our schools to full flower. I fear, however, that our schools as we had them in Russia will not return, any more than will the *Forstei* service. My concerns on that account are doubtless superfluous.

* * * *

I strongly disputed the generally accepted view that there was no place for a conscience on the Alt Berdjaner *Forstei*. However, I was soon to be put to a demanding test which ended by flouting the law. The authorities had made a determined attempt to make the service hard [55] for the Mennonites. It had been ordered, for example, that no draftee was allowed to go home on leave even if a member of the family lay ill or died. A leave like that would have made no difference to the *Forstei* since the whole service was useless anyway. However, the soldiers at the front had to stay there regardless of what happened at home, and therefore we too had to stay and tend our acacias. It seemed senseless and cruel to us that for the sake of those acacias we should be separated from someone who was dying. Indeed, it seemed to be a mockery, and so the law was generally disregarded without any trace of conscientious scruple.

We were cutting wood in the so-called "Slave-Driver Section" when suddenly I saw a pair of familiar brown horses coming along the clearing. They were my own horses and my cart driven by a man who had come to tell me that in the previous night my wife had given birth to a daughter, but now lay deathly ill in the hospital and wanted to see me. What to do? The working-day was nearly over, and I had fulfilled my quota for the day. The government would not lose a thing if I went home for the night, and I could easily be back to work in the morning. At home my wife lay near death, but the law was clear: I had to stay in the barracks. The *starshii* happened to be in our quarter. I asked him what I should do. "I cannot give you permission to go home," he said, pulling me into a more private place. "You know that as well as I do. However, until early the day after tomorrow, I won't notice if you are not here." I struggled briefly, shut my eyes, jumped onto the cart as I was, and drove off. Strange, the way the Altonau poplars rustled as I drove by.

When I arrived at the hospital, the crisis was already over, and my wife and I thanked God for His gracious aid. I remained to chat with her until about ten o'clock and then thrashed about on my bed in restless sleep until three in the morning. By daybreak I was back in the *Forstei* to continue my all-important tasks there. Thus I myself experienced how hard it is to obey laws which lack any rational basis, or to obey when in those days "dodging" (leaving work surreptitiously) was so common that it could not be controlled. The foolishness of the exclusive [56] laws and regulations to which we were subject was to blame for a lot of the trouble.

This Mennonite heritage with its advantages and its impediments, with its bright light and its dark shadows, this is the field on which I work and from which the substantial characters emerged which so impressed me. Here Johannes Stein[11] resolved his inner conflict and found light, on which Agatha grew to be a supple, strong and mature person and fell in love with Herman Jäger, and on which Peta Panna strove for his portion of modest happiness and never found it. This is the authentic Mennonite reality that I love so deeply, to which I am faithfully committed until I die, even when, occasionally, it scolds or even despises me. I will always work for this heritage, stressing its sunny aspects and scolding its dark faults. I will publicly expose and pillory its follies, but also carefully lift the veil of its profound spirituality so that people will see it blaze forth from the darkness like a precious gem.

When I began my service on the Alt Berdjaner *Forstei*, in September, 1915, there was first a difficult farewell at home, and then jolly greetings in the *Forstei*, insofar as that was possible under the circumstances. A number of teachers arrived there with me, who were soon dubbed the *Gegrommten* by the rest. Every philologist should have to spend time in the *Forstei*. Here he could properly observe the emergence of a language, or the transition from one language to another. The conscripts came from far and near and brought all their peculiarities together into a new mix and gave their banter free rein. And around the *Forstei*, the largely Russian world observed this tightly enclosed Mennonite society, and added some of its own spice to its growth and development.

The special word mentioned above developed as follows: in the Russian language a *gramotny* (from *grammotta*, writing) is one who is able to read and write in contrast to an illiterate, a *negramotny*. Out of the Russian adjective *gramotny* the *Forstei* boys eventually derived the

---

[11] Johannes Stein, Agatha, Herman Jäger, and Peta Panna are characters from Janzen's novels.

German verb *"gromme,"* that is, to make someone into a *gramotny.* Whenever someone did something that was really too stupid, it would be said, *"Den woa wie woll noch emaol en bet gromme motte."* ["We will just have to *gromme* that one a bit."] This *gromme* developed according to a method of which neither Pestalozzi[12] nor Amos Comenius[13] had ever dreamt. From the verb *gromme* was derived the participle *gegrommt,* and that was made into the noun "the *Gegrommte*" by adding the definite article.

Smoke rises out of the chimney. Occasionally it rises in a powerful burst. It would be obvious, therefore, to say of a person who quickly left the room, that he came "smoking out". Now, if a person can come "smoking out," I would like to know why it is not possible for someone to go [57] "smoking in". And indeed, it was possible. The man who held the position of the *dezhurnii po kazarme* was normally called *Stienke* in the *Forstei.* He did what at home the housemaids did, who often had the name of Justina or *Stienke* [a diminutive of *Justina*]. It happened that *Stienke* was carrying a container of ashes to the ashpit. As he emptied it, he came too close to the edge and plunged headlong into the pit, sending up a cloud of ashes like smoke out of a chimney. Two "scabs," that is, malingerers, who were possibly quite well but had reported in sick in order finally to have a "dry" day, stood there thoughtfully and observed *Stienke*'s descent into the ashpit. "That one smoked in," said the one with unshakeable tranquillity. "What if instead of ashes there had been a lot of knives down there?" ventured the other. "Then he would have knifed in," replied the first one as *Stienke* struggled out of the pit into the light of day, coughing and sputtering. The "scabs" observed him nonchalantly but made no move to give him a hand on the way out. Two priceless words with new meanings and value had been introduced into the world there at the edge of the Alt Berdjaner ashpit. Henceforth, if someone got into difficulty of a moderate degree, he was said to have smoked in. If, however, he landed in really big trouble, he was said to have knifed in.

---

[12] Johann Heinrich Pestalozzi, (1746-1827), Swiss educational theorist and innovator, well-known among Russian Mennonites.

[13] Johann Amos Comenius (Komensky), (1592-1670), the founder of the modern theory of education, and much loved by Mennonites in Europe.

Everyone knows that a *Berg* [mountain] is a mountain. However, if there is an assembly of many high peaks, it is known as *Gebirge* [mountains]. A pool is *Wasser* [water]. Even a *nichtgegrommte* knows this. But if many large pools come together it is known as *Gewässer* [waters]. Even the *nichtgegrommte* person is playfully aware that the prefix *ge-* increases the value of the word. For precisely this reason a *Prannick* (gingerbread cookie) is a *Prannick*. But a very large, beautiful *Prannick* is a *Geprannick*. An ordinary motorbike is a *Motocyklet*. But a very good, so to speak, excellent motorbike is a *Motogecyklet*. Etc., etc., etc.

Chapter 6

Liudinka

About Christmas our *starshii* called an assembly and told us that the *ratniki* [soldiers] and the "scabs" would be transferred, some to the Crimea and the rest to somewhere in the north. No one knew precisely where that would be. Lists would be prepared.

While the lists were being prepared, a number of the service men tried to influence their place on the list, but most just hung their heads and waited idly for what was to come. We already knew that the *Forsteis* of the north, [58] like those in the Crimea, were more places of exile than of service, and that many Russian officials would be pleased if we simply died there. What was in store for us?

Those who had the good fortune of going to the Crimea were at least not far from home and could occasionally "dodge" out. But those who were headed north generally found themselves in difficult circumstances. In addition, we did not even know precisely what the destination of those going north was, and did not know it even when we left. Legally we were not allowed to get Christmas leave, but now even our old forester, His Excellency Siwietzky, winked at the law. On Christmas Eve all that could be seen was the dust of the *ratniki* and the *destwitel'ny* [labourers] heading home.

After the holidays the bell called us to the dining hall, where the lists were read. It was divided fairly between the *gegrommte* and the *nichtgegrommte*. From each group about half went south and the other half north. Many of my good friends were smoked in and had to go to the Crimea. I with many others was knifed in and was sent north. But where to? We were told only that we were to be sent to Kursk,[1] to be available to the Kursk-Orlov administration of the imperial domains. There we would be given further instructions about our destination.

For New Year's Day we "dodged" home again with the connivance of the forester in order to prepare ourselves for the long journey and the long absence from home. Whatever should one take and what leave behind? Had we known what was waiting for us, we could have prepared. As it was, we were pretty well at a loss. Whoever had money, took it. Whoever lacked it, surrendered himself to fate or to God, depending upon his belief or unbelief. I sold my horses, divided the proceeds with my family, and left early on January 2, 1916, for Melitopol, from where we would be transported by train.

It was a difficult road I began to walk that day, but we were comforted by a word the Lord gave us in our morning worship. The children were still sleeping. "Mother Lena," as she was popularly known because of her position as head of the dormitory at the Girls' School, sat across from me at the breakfast table, her big brown eyes filled with tears. I took down the little book *Strength for the Day* and opened it up to January 2. There it was: "He led them by a straight way, till they reached a city [59] to dwell in" (Psalm 107:7). The table was richly spread; we still had more than we needed. It was loaded with what had been prepared for the holidays. But neither of us, anticipating our first major separation, was hungry, and we hardly touched all the good food. God's Word, however, had comforted and strengthened us. We were not running blindly into the arms of fate, but were led by a loving Father on the right way to a city where we could dwell. The road there became very long and difficult, and my Lena finally succumbed to it in exhaustion. But she reclined into the arms of her Saviour and thus arrived sooner than I at the city where we can dwell in peace and in rest.

---

[1] Kursk is about 625 km north of Melitopol.

In Melitopol no one knew about our orders to go north or wanted to provide us with the necessary cars. That at least is what we were told. At the same time they told us that a late arrival at Kursk could have very negative consequences for us since, after all, it was wartime. They regretted it, but claimed not to be able to help us because the necessary papers had not been sent to the administration of the station on time. In short, they expected us conscripts to grease their palms. But they had not counted on our determination.

We simply turned our backs on them, went into the waiting room, and with difficulty found a free spot on a windowsill. There, *gegrommt* as we were, we prepared a submission to the station commandant on the basis of the documents we carried by number and address in which we described our circumstances briefly, but clearly. After handing in the document, properly notarized by our office, we were firmly determined to set up house in the station at Melitopol until it should please them to send us on our way.

It did not, however, actually come to the submission of the document. One of the civilian officers of the station suddenly hurried into the waiting room, came over to us, and informed us that the cars for our transport were ready. Apparently the officials had noted that we did not personally care if we left or not, that they could not intimidate us, and that they would receive no bribes from us for the cars. So we tore up our carefully prepared submission to the station commandant and embarked in the cattle cars that had quickly been transformed into passenger cars by equipping them with iron stoves.

So we had our cars with the stoves, and some fuel was delivered. Should there not be enough, we could always beg for some coal from the locomotive engineer, or, in a pinch, we could steal some when the train stopped. If we fired the stoves, which were far too big for the small cars, we were in danger of being roasted. If we did not, we could not survive in the bitter cold which soon set in. One night our car nearly went up in flames because one of the comrades [60], waking up half frozen, had fired the stove before he lay down again.

In Kursk we learned that we were to go to the mountain forest of Briansk,[2] where several small groups of Mennonites were already working. The news that we had received from there did not sound encouraging. I had especially heard that the forester of the Snyeshetz Forstei resented the detachment there and that he harassed it in every possible way. We were to go beyond Snyeshetzkoye and Briansk past Shukovka to Ljudinka. Some of the *destwitel'ny* had already been sent there, and these too had not reported much that was good.

Farther and farther the train took us across the endless snow fields of Russia. At first we saw the little Russian villages lying along the rail line with their whitewashed clay huts (*khaty*). Low and flat, they appeared to be holding onto the earth. Only the poplars rose high above the low roofs. A ring of windmills surrounded the villages. They became smaller and shabbier, the farther north we went.

North of Kharkov we drove through the deciduous forest. Then followed open fields on which villages lay scattered. But the houses here were of a different type. They too were whitewashed, but they were wood structures. The walls are constructed of wattle covered with clay and carefully sealed. Whitewashed, it looks like a clay wall. However, the walls are not very sturdy, so they tend to buckle. Most of the houses lean one way or another.

North of Kursk the forest became more dense. It was now coniferous. The houses in the villages here were built of logs and covered with thin boards or shingles. We saw no more *khaty*. These were *izby*, known to us from stories and pictures, but we had not seen them before. Here we felt physically that we were going farther and farther into foreign country. Into the foreign country towards an unknown destination. Where was it? What would it be like there?

In Orel our cars were switched to the Riga-Orlov track, and we drove farther and farther into the dark Russian forest. It was slow going. "*Tjische jedjesch, daljsche budjesch,*" said one of the men who was looking out of the window in a thoughtful mood. That is a Russian

---

[2] Briansk is about 165 km northwest of Kursk.

proverb and means: "The slower you travel, the farther [61] you get." But the word *tjische* means not only "slower" but also "quieter." Another of the *gegrommte* sat on the upper bunk next to him. After a time of quiet, serious reflection he said, turning the proverb around, "*Daljsche jedjesh, tjische budjesch.*" Translated that means: "The farther you travel, the quieter you become." Then we were all quiet for quite a while until someone in a corner began singing *Thy way and all thy sorrows*. One after the other joined in. Loudly and confidently we sang "Bid farewell to your sorrows, and to your cares goodnight!" For our own comfort we continued with *Befiehl du deine Wege* [*Leave all to His direction*]. We sang the whole hymn verse by verse, and fervently we harmonized the last verse:

> *Give, Lord, the consummation to all our hearts distress;*
> *Our hands, our feet, O strengthen; in death our spirits bless.*
> *Thy truth and thy protection for evermore we pray:*
> *With these in heavenly glory shall end our certain way.*[3]

* * * *

Finally we arrived. Liudinka is a little nest in the heart of the forest. Wolves and bears are no fairy tales here; rather, they constitute a considerable plague for the residents. Two sawmills had been built near the little village. The one belonged to the massive Briansk locomotive factories; the other had belonged to a certain Prince Olsufiev, but had then become government property. Our work was to supply these mills with logs. Our forester was a young Pole. They said he was quite tolerable when he had his hat pushed back on his head, but terrible when he darkly pulled it down over his forehead. He was the one to whom we were handed over for good or ill.

For the time being, however, he was not to be seen. His assistant, who in the language of the *Forstei* was called *Pietzker*, came to meet us. A pitiful subaltern: you could see it in his eyes as well as by the seams of

---

[3] *Befiehl du deine Wege*, a hymn by Paul Gerhard. It had twelve stanzas. The translation is taken from the *Mennonite Hymnal*, 1969, #338.

his somewhat worn greatcoat with the polished eagle buttons. He was polite and helpful, but could offer us little. He did show us the way to the huts which from now on were to be our barracks. The majority of the detachment trotted away with him from the station. Some of our luggage followed – no – preceded on sleighs. It would have been risky to have them follow.

I remained as watchman with the rest of the stuff at the station. A crowd of curious Liudinka citizens had quickly [62] gathered around me. Without any embarrassment they began to discuss and evaluate the pile of suitcases and boxes, as well as our detachment and the effect of our arrival in the village. At first I acted as though I understood nothing of the conversation. In Melitopol I had bought a shiny, raven-black leather suit. In this uniform I now walked with dignity back and forth near our possessions. When the crowd approached too closely, I walked right around the suitcases so that the curious had to make way for me and thus move back from the baggage. All of this happened outside. The sky was overcast and crumbs of snow fell slowly. It was not warm.

The people here spoke a somewhat affected, northern dialect, in which the name *Ivan* sounded like *Yavan*. The language sounded strange and comical. And the clothing! the coffee-coloured *yarmulkes* and *sierjaki*, the fur hats well-trimmed by moths. The only thing they had in common was that they all had a hollow that could be tilted over the coiffure; otherwise they were pointed, flat, round, angular, tall, low and whatever else. And the huge bark shoes that encased the ends of their thin legs that were wrapped in sacks and laced with thick string. None of this looked very impressive at first glance.

More and more often I had to make the circuit around the hill of luggage because the inquisitive crowd became more and more pushy. "What kind of folk do you think they are, Yavan?" said one. Yavan, a slight chap, whose head sat on his long thin neck like a pumpkin on a broom stick, crossed his hand over his chest, ceremonially put his heavy bark-shoed foot forward, pulled on his stumpy pipe, spat on the ground, clamped his eyes on my mound of bags with dignity and covetousness, and began: "These are people . . . . they sleep, . . . and naturally, they also eat, . . . and . . . ." He added other bodily functions which I don't feel like

repeating. "Yavan, O Yavan, what do they call them? Menn, menn . . .?"
"Menn, menn! You are a menn yourself! They are Dynamites, Dy-na-
mites! Get it?"

He was quite serious about it. For him there was so little difference
between Mennonites and Dynamites that he had never noticed his
mistake. He understood the one as little as the other. He had correctly
grasped that they were both quite dangerous. The priest had warned them
emphatically about the Mennonites, and the soldiers always spoke about
dynamite as of something terribly dangerous. No wonder that it appeared
to Yavan [63] that the priest and the soldiers were talking more or less
about the same thing, something dangerous and harmful. In a word, the
Dynamites, one of whom was walking back and forth in front of him,
black and shining. Obviously he was better informed about political
economy than about confessional and sectarian matters. He continued: "I
will tell you what their arrival in Liudinka will mean for the *mushik*
(farmer). Bread, which for so long has been five kopeks a pound, will now
rise to seven kopeks, and for the dozen *Kringel*[4] which you could until
now buy for ten kopeks, you will from now on have to pay fifteen."
"Hohooooooe," drawled Yermolai who had asked the question. "A fine
kettle of fish!" (*Eto ne delo*) the others chimed in. "That will never do, no
way! But what's to be done, Yavan?" "Take a big stick and kill the lot,"
said Yavan without hesitation.

In Liudinka, too, questions about what shall we eat? what shall we
drink? were the first order of business. Moreover, they were willing to
solve their social and economic problems as simply as was done by the
ruling cabinets in Petersburg, Berlin, London, Paris and wherever else.
What could ever embarrass the person who knows that he can playfully
solve every problem with murder? Yavan's words echoed in the hearts of
his hearers. They looked at me threateningly and moved closer to my
suitcases.

The moment had come for me to show some courage, which actually
caused me no great difficulty. Boldly I advanced on them and
demonstrated that I too could speak and understand Russian. They

---

[4] A twisted white roll.

retreated in surprise, and with an embarrassed smile Yavan assured me that he had said all of that just for fun and that they had not the slightest intention of laying hands on us. As he kept retreating, a small boy got in the way of his heels, and he was glad to have found a convenient deflector. Stumbling, he grabbed the boy by the collar and yelled "*Pyetka, otkhodi!*" (Beat it, Pete!). Then he turned to me as to an old acquaintance and said familiarly, "You just can't trust them." And then, with angry, blazing eyes, he turned again to Pyetka: "*Ty Pyetka. Smotri y menya!*" (You, Pete! Look out!) And then had come the convenient moment to call to his comrades: "*A nam, rebyata, pora!*" ("Time to go, children.") And off they went, gesticulating and talking avidly to each other.

For a long time my comrades did not return, and my feet got cold. But then, what's so special about that in wartime? Finally several of the sleighs came back. We loaded [64] the luggage and headed for our quarters. I had imagined that they would not be palatial, but I certainly did not expect that the hovels would be so miserable. On frozen board bunks from which we first had to remove the snow and ice with a hatchet, we prepared our night lodging. After that several of us set about to get a fire started in the stove. As is customary with stoves, it began with great billows of smoke, but soon began to radiate a comfortable warmth, and also to bring the water for our tea to a boil in its cavernous depths. All of us had toasted *Zwieback* and Christmas cookies in our suitcases, so the evening meal did warm us through, and we began to feel better.

So much better, indeed, that some of us became quite high-spirited and ventured that we needed to have straw for our mattresses, although we could imagine that straw would be hard to find in this woodland. I should not have been among these exuberant spirits, but I was, and with several others, left to find some straw. But no straw was to be had in this desperate village. Finally one of the *muzhiks* directed us to the village *kulak* (village "fist," i.e., village usurer) who bore the descriptive name *Resunov*, which means butcher. "He has everything," said our adviser, and pointed us in the direction of the usurer's house. We found him to be not as bad as the *muzhik* had described him. And he had straw, but it was in a hut some distance into the forest. No matter. We wanted straw. He hitched up in the dark and drove out into the forest with us, where he carefully weighed out some rye straw for us on a pocket scale, took payment for it then and there, and hauled it over to our barracks.

It had not been easy, but we now had the advantage of being the envied ones in our quarters. A problem surfaced, however, when bedtime came. Our filled straw mattresses would not go into the narrow space to which we were limited on the bunk. A perplexing dilemma! But we solved it by giving our neighbours some of the straw, packing the mattresses together, and squeezing them down by lying on them. They had to fit themselves into the space provided, and we had a layer of straw, albeit a thin one, between us and the cold, hard boards.

It was all accepted in good humour, but it was not hard to become serious again for our evening worship. Seriousness was always closer to us than laughter. Not because of our situation, oh no. For those in the trenches were far worse [65] off than we, and we could be thankful for the good that had still come our way. Our concerns were for our loved ones at home. They were subject to the liquidation law[5] and were threatened with resettlement. We had witnessed what had happened to the resettled Germans from Volhynia. The governor of Kharkov, a certain Koshchuro-Massalisky, let their children starve to death at a time when there was still bread to spare in Russia. Go and visit the German cemetery in Kharkov and find the graves of the Volhynian children who died of hunger in 1915, and who were buried twelve at a time in a single grave.

The Mennonites have always been loyal to the Russian government even in the hardest times they experienced in Russia. The injustices and

---

[5] This law was part of a massive campaign initiated by Imperial Russia during World War I against its German and Mennonite subjects. Suddenly all German newspapers were banned, in spite of their unqualified support of the Tsar. By 1914 the government had also abandoned its practice of separating Mennonites from Germans. From this point on they were treated with the same suspicion. Restrictions against the empire's "German" population increased as the Russian army faltered, and culminated in a series of expropriation measures directed against all German landholding. The most repressive decree was issued by Tsar Nicholas on 6 February 1917, and would have obliterated all German and Mennonite landholdings if enacted. Under these circumstances, it is hardly surprising that Mennonites were jubilant at the news of the Tsar's abdication less than three weeks later, during the so-called February revolution.

violations that were committed by the imperial government against citizens of German nationality although no disloyalty could be proved against them, produced a chilling of the love for that government. As a result Mennonites, too, breathed easier when the February Revolution broke out and the government, which had threatened to let our wives and children perish miserably because they were of German extraction, was turned out.[6]

When the massive betrayal of *Miaso-yedov*[7] (the name means meat-eater) was uncovered, government officials were much concerned to show that this *Miaso-yedov* was German. For the "honour" of Germans like Schwarz, Stürmer, Schmidt and others who became Slavophiles, this must be mentioned here. The priest Gregorii Petrov was so carried away by his hate that he wrote about the Germans in Russia as "devil's seed" (*sataninskoe semia*) to stir up hate against those against whom not a shred of disloyalty could be proved. We will also "fondly" remember the Cossacks who, on the orders of the government, looked for aircraft and zeppelins in our dresser drawers.

In January, 1905 the Russian workers lost their faith in the *Tsar-Batiuschka* (father-tsar), [a diminutive term of endearment]. In February, 1915, the Mennonites lost that faith as well. When in February, 1917, the tsarist regime was toppled, they breathed a sigh of relief.

* * * *

In Liudinka we found an organization already in place, created by the *destvitel'ny*. They had been sent here because they knew how to set up a *Forstei* [66] and had arrived shortly before we did. Already there was a twenty-five-year-old *starshii* who was ready and willing to command

---

[6] The February Revolution culminated in Nicholas II's abdication from the throne in early 1917. Janzen here suggests that Mennonites, along with most other members of Imperial Russian society, welcomed the news. Mennonites were far more alarmed by the Bolshevik Revolution of October, 1917, which promised a very different future for them.

[7] The *Miaso-edov* may refer to one of countless rumours from this period that portrayed all Germans as traitors. Janzen rejects this characterization when he refers to Germans as Slavophiles, or lovers of the Russian land and its people.

forty-year-olds. There were also bakers and cooks and whatever belongs to a well-ordered household. All we had to do was to submit to the already-existing order, and do our outdoor work.

But to command forty-year-olds was not as simple as it may appear at first glance. In time, changes were introduced after which, so far as I can recall, only the chief cook and one baker remained in their posts. I honestly and readily admit that we *ratniki* liberally exploited our numerical advantage during the implementation of these changes and suppressed the *destvitel'ny* on the principle "I am big and you are small." Politics are politics and in politics, power and horse-trading are the norm. That was no different in the Mennonite detachment of Liudinka than in Berlin, Petersburg, Paris, London, etc.

When the ferment in the detachment had come to an end I found myself in the role of kitchen choreboy. At first they had wanted to give me the honourable position of economist of the detachment. Now, although I am capable of behaving quite badly, this time I was honest enough to admit that I could not even properly manage my own money, let alone the money of others. So they demoted me to kitchen choreboy with the proviso that I should be free on Saturday afternoon. For I had also been appointed the preacher for the unit and had to have time to prepare my Sunday sermon. In neither of these offices did I achieve anything notable. Again I must thank my colleagues, several of whom had come to the camp as ministerial candidates, and who participated actively in pastoral work even though they were compelled to do heavy work out in the forest. Later on, older ministers, who were also conscripted, came to Liudinka and helped extensively in the care of souls and preaching.

As kitchen choreboy I spent time splitting green wood and attempted to find a method of making green wood burn, but without notable success. Had not our chief cook, the always easy-going Unger, been better at it than I, we should likely, even today, not be ready with our first pot of borscht.

Actually, there was no kitchen, and our utensils consisted of a kettle that was too small and an iron rod. So, with relatively small effort, we dug a deep hole in a snowbank near the door of the dining hall. With the help of our iron bar and two poles we built a tripod, hung our kettle on it, and threw in meat, water, potatoes, [67] and a few other ingredients. While this mixture was slowly freezing on top, we attempted to get a fire going below with green wood. At the same time we were conjecturing whether perhaps the same changes in the food would take place from frost as from heat. In that case the preparation of food in Liudinka would have been greatly simplified. Unfortunately, we could not come to a satisfactory conclusion with those calculations either.

In digging the hole in the snowdrift, we had planned that in this way our fire would be protected from wind. It was. But we had not anticipated that the busy Liudinka wind in cooperation with the inexhaustible Liudinka clouds would be tirelessly determined to shovel the snow all back into the hole. We had not noticed that wind and clouds had been watching us idly but with interest as we were digging. When we were done, and just as the first stick began to burn and our soup had a centimetre of ice on its surface, they believed their time had come and, as a test case, threw a small load of snow on kettle and fire. "Well, well," said Unger who had been stretched out on all fours in front of the non-existent stove door and blowing on a nearly non-existent fire. He sat up, brushed the snow off his neck, and looked up. At that precise moment the second load of snow fell into our hole, and we understood that looking into the clouds would be of no use here. We had to act, but how?

The far end of our enclosure was blocked off by a barn and a large shed. Resolutely Unger said: "Come!" Immediately I caught his intention. We ran over, took off all the doors we could find, and dragged them to our fire in order to block off the entry of snow and wind to our precious hole. Now Unger, with his superb ability, was able to get a fire going, and when the men came back from work hungry, the ice crust on our soup had nearly melted. There was some grumbling but it was not intolerably loud or obtrusive. The lads understood that it was not so easy all at once to build a kitchen, dry the firewood, and cook the soup, and so again they tucked into the provisions they had brought with them from home.

We, however, stayed with our job of preparing the soup. The potatoes were already done, but not the meat. "It must have been an old cow," said Unger. The potatoes began to turn into mashed potatoes, [68] and the meat was still uncooked and tough. Everything in the soup except for the perverse meat turned to mush. Finally, however, what should have been lunch was ready as supper, and the men could come and get their rations. I stood at the kettle and served the soup into their bowls. Then, before everyone had received a portion, a deputation from the dining hall appeared and put to me the question as to what it was that we were enjoying for supper. I looked at them severely and returned the question: could they not figure it out for themselves? No, came the reply, they were not *gegrommt* enough for that. "Well," I said, "why not ask Unger. He is chief cook." But the judgement was that he was not *gegrommt* enough either. Being *gegrommt* can, under some circumstances, be quite catastrophic. Guys," I said after some reflection, "I did not bring my encyclopedia. Tell you what I'll do. I'll write home, ask them to check it, and send me the decision. Then come and see me again." They found that agreeable and went back into the dining hall. As they went I heard one of them mutter: "Encyclopedia -edia -edia, the *gegrommte* don't know what they feed-ia." In this manner the first food I helped cook at Liudinka awakened the Muse; her kiss inspired one of the conscripts to be a poet. Yes, all beginnings are hard.

* * * *

One day while I was working again in our hole in the snow, bent over and blowing on the fire, I had the distinct feeling that someone was standing above me, watching me. I looked up, and became aware of a tall man of perhaps thirty in high boots, leather jacket and a military hat standing at the edge of our kitchen cave. He wore a small black moustache. His hat was pushed back on his head and he looked down on me pleasantly. Immediately I recognized him as my superior, the forester. I clicked my heels, grabbed my spoon in my left and saluted him in the proper form with my right hand. He waved away the formality and greeted me as man to man. "Are you the chief cook?" he asked. "No," I replied, "I am the kitchen choreboy." He laughed, and continued: "Are you not the preacher in this detachment?" "At your service, right honourable sir; it is my sub-office." "Tell me, please," he asked, "who actually are the Mennonites?" Looking up out of my snow cave at my audience, standing in the steam of my bubbling soup, stirring spoon in left hand, I gave a lecture on

Mennonitism; its [69] history, extent and character, not forgetting to mention the gracious good will of the Polish kings who gave shelter to the Mennonites on their lands because they had recognized and valued their sobriety and industry as farmers.

"Can't you come up out of that hole?" the forester finally asked in some impatience. I threw an embarrassed glance in the direction of the pot. The forester's eyes swept the enclosure and then called our *starshii* by name. I heard heels clicking and the proper words of address to the forester. "Send another man here immediately!" he ordered. The *starshii* was clearly perplexed, not knowing where to get such a person. He hesitated while the forester looked at him, then with a jerk, pulled his hat down onto the bridge of his nose. What an effect a little tug on the cap can have when the one wearing the hat has the necessary authority. "Yes sir! At your service, most honourable sir!" As he said the words he turned, and in a few moments Unger stood before me and took the spoon out of my hand. I ascended out of the cave into the light of day.

"Sagursky," said the forester, introducing himself, and reached for my hand. As good friends we went hence. While I was sitting with the forester in his quarters drinking tea, I heard the dinner bell ringing, and remembered the apt words of Friedrich Schiller:

> *Freed of all his duties,*
> *The apprentice hears the vesper bell;*
> *The master labours on alone.*[8]

Unger, who was always amiable, was probably thinking and expressing unkind thoughts about his irresponsible kitchen choreboy. But no doubt there would be those who would comfort him with the words: "He is smoked out and you are knifed in. That is the way it is in the service of the crown." But that was how I was relieved of my menial service and came into the forester's *bashlyk* which means, in the language of the *Forstei*, that I had wormed my way into his good favour. I was made the camp's manager of rough logs.

---

[8] "Ledig aller Pflicht hört der Bursch die Vesper schlagen. Meister muss sich immer plagen." From *Das Lied von der Glocke*.

But this appointment gave me the desperate feeling of having been knifed in. For I am no business man, but was now required to manage a camp, to receive the logs from the forest and then deliver them from the camp to the sawmill. Every evening I had to give the forester an exact inventory.

Evening, 3 March there were in the camp	xxx logs
Received, 4 March	yyy logs
Total	zzz logs [70]
Delivered to the mill	ttt logs
As of 5 March, in the camp	uuu logs

That would have been relatively easy had not the *muzhiks* who brought the logs in, and the *desiatnik* who received the logs at the mill, always been determined to swindle me.

The drivers demanded that I record the logs they delivered as one inch thicker than they actually were. That would increase their fee as drivers which, they opined, would make not a shred of difference to the crown. I myself would then be responsible for getting from wherever possible logs of sufficient thickness so that the deception would not be noticed. Once they began to wheedle at the gate, they could be got rid of only by swearing loudly even if one was not angry. As long as one did not swear, they felt they had hope of achieving something with their begging. I could not and would not swear.

The following morning the *desiatnik* who managed the store of cut lumber arrived punctually and claimed that I had recorded more logs than had arrived at the mill. The man received a very modest wage and tried to augment his meagre financial circumstances by increasing his income honestly with small thefts from the store of cut lumber. This was difficult to conceal if the number of logs delivered were correctly recorded. He always tried to get credit from me for a few of them.

I simply could not do it; I had no gift for it. I would much rather have been kitchen choreboy under Unger's gentle rule, especially since the forester had given us a kitchen with a roof and enough large kettles. But it never came to that.

* * * *

A government drugstore had been established in the camp for the many in our detachment who were sick, as well as for the other workers in the factory nearby. It was located in a separate house along with several beds for the seriously ill. The forester transferred me there upon my request after he had relieved me of my duties as camp manager, also on my request. Once I had handed the camp over to my successor, also a *gegrommte*, I was even more relieved than I had been when I had advanced from kitchen choreboy to camp manager.

In my drugstore I was sole ruler, since the authority which Gerassim Pavlovich, the military medic in Liudinka, exercised over me was not hard to bear. The man was happy when anyone took over some of his work and was not put off by his occasional bad moods. The forester was always courteous and fair with me, even when I was no longer his friend as a result of having had [71] a major quarrel with him concerning several sick men.

After I had taken over the drugstore a new education began for me. As preacher I continued to be responsible for the welfare and discipline of the community even though the nature of the work here was quite different from that in the Girls' School or in the church at home. I was still required to care for souls.

But now I was also to care for the physical welfare and health of those committed to me, for there was no physician for many miles around. In particular, Gerassim Pavlovich could not be considered as psychotherapist for our detachment, for among his own people he exercised this part of his work in a manner to which we were not accustomed. Our view was that for the treatment to be effective, the patient must first learn to trust the physician. Gerassim Pavlovich counted respect more important than trust, and so his whole manner always elicited respect more readily than trust. Our fellows had remarkably little respect, and so his methods did not work with us. Thus, more fell to me to do than was proper.

It was often quite tricky to navigate the shoals that surrounded me. The "scabs" wanted "dry" days, but such requests demanded that I lie, complete with seal and signature. I could not lie, and so there were often disgruntled faces. The forester wanted as few on the sick list as possible. When I pointed out that there would always be some sick men since the *Forsteis* in the south always got rid first of those who were sick and incompatible when men were moved to other camps, his response was that that was none of his concern. He had, he said, no desire to do anyone an injustice or to torment anyone. But the administration of the imperial domains had sent these men to him as healthy and able to work. Excusing them from work would be interpreted as criticism of the measures of the government, and this he, as a subordinate, could not afford to do. It was his obligation somehow to use to advantage the manpower which had been put at his disposal. You had to give him credit; he knew his work, and tried to strike a profit out of this crown endeavour.

From time to time I had to travel with a group of sick men to Briansk. They were to be inspected by a commission. The chairman of this commission was always the royal marshall of the district. Several physicians had to diagnose the ailments and recommend whether the men should be discharged or sent back to service. I never had any idea who our royal marshall was, for he never said or did anything of importance. He fulfilled his function by simply being there. But I shall never forget one of the doctors whose name was Krivorottov, which means something like "crooked mouth." With mocking laughter he sent every Mennonite back [72] to service with the remark that, after all, they were not in the war, but in the forest in a spa. They did not need to be discharged even though they had a legal right to it. There was no point in bringing even seriously ill men before this commission unless the visit could be planned to coincide with the absence of Krivorottov. The other physicians were more just to us and had more good will.

In our detachment we had three men with serious epilepsy. On one occasion one of them, in an attack of madness, fled from the railway car [in which he was working] and wandered aimlessly about the forest until he was finally found lying unconscious by some Russian soldiers from a nearby garrison who returned him to us. Because he was a Mennonite, he was not discharged from the service. But these commissions were not calculated to increase the love of Mennonites for the imperial government. They remained loyal to it until it was overthrown, because they had once pledged their allegiance. But when that government was deposed, they shed no tear for it.

It was my good fortune that the forester had always been fair and remained so. I doubt that he really regarded us highly, let alone loved us. But I fear that we did not much deserve to be loved. At the beginning there was a certain warmth in his attitude towards us. But one day, we and the Greek Catholics were given the day off because it was one of the saint's days, which for religious reasons we were not obligated to observe since Mennonites do not venerate any saints. On this day the forester requested the detachment to serve as beaters for a bear hunt. He did not give an order; he requested. Virtually no one showed up on the parade ground when the steam whistle called the assembly. From that day on all warmth disappeared from his attitude toward us, and I will not blame him for it. He believed that he deserved some sense of obligation toward him, and we should have demonstrated it. He was not to blame for the injustices of the government and had, within the limits of his position, proved friendly toward us. However, although the cordiality toward us was no longer there, he was always fair.

Our Mennonite separateness has much to be said for it, but it has the disadvantage that we do not always feel obligated toward non-Mennonites even though in everyday life we are closely linked to them. It appeared to me occasionally that we had not properly understood the saying about "being in the world but not of the world." Our manner of living was often not "in heaven" but very frequently, as we excluded our non-Mennonite neighbours, "alongside the world." In fact, we believed that we stood above them, and that they were obligated to serve us with privileges from on high since, [73] as prudent people and respectable farmers, we were naturally entitled to them. We were therefore surprised when, after that bear hunt, the friendliness of our forester was suddenly gone. Were we not the same respectable people and in our hearts the same solid farmers that we were before the bear hunt, although, of course, our industriousness in agriculture was for the time being in abeyance?

True, in the sawmill and in the whole camp operation, we did good work and would have fared well in any competition. The forester understood that and gave us our work accordingly. He appreciated the true value of our diligence and won out in a dispute that developed over this issue after the bear hunt, and succeeded in rescinding an order for the detachment to work on Sunday, which had been imposed as punishment.

Chapter 7

Standing in the Whirlwind

On an evening when the north wind blew against the windows of the forestry house, I sat with the forester near his fireplace over a cup of tea. He was as amiable as ever, and treated me as his equal. He told me about his experiences at the shrine of the Mother of God at Chenstochau [Czestochova in Poland]. He had once fallen on his knees before the image of the Mother of God despite the fact that he did not believe in much. He explained it as a function of the hypnotic power over the masses produced by the carefully constructed environment. He had not been able to resist it. Pleasantly chatting, he went on to the subject of the significance of the church for the state. He gave it as his opinion that the milieu which the church created, thanks to its power over the masses, could be very useful but also very detrimental for the functioning of the state. No wonder, therefore, that sometimes the state persecutes and sometimes supports the church. In this relationship the state is governed strictly by utilitarian self-interest. Precisely for this reason the Polish king Sigismund had granted the Mennonites freedom for their religious beliefs, notwithstanding that these kings were fervent Catholics and as such were actually obligated to turn heretics, which is what the Mennonites were in the eyes of the Catholics, over to the Inquisition.[1]

The forester supposed that as leader of a congregation I likely had a lot of experience with the power a *cultus* can exert over the masses, and that therefore only certain causes would have to be produced in order to yield certain effects, also, he parenthetically observed, in this detachment. That would be very welcome for him as forester, for it would allow him to accomplish with kindness in his command what was extracted only with harshness in, for example, Snyeshetzkaia. And, again parenthetically, he added that such a procedure would suit him perfectly, for he was against all [74] oppression and coercion. He fell silent and blew great clouds of smoke from his short pipe towards the fireplace.

I took a swallow from my tea glass and began to chat in turn. Indeed, many are the effects worked upon the human heart. Some of them can be traced back to their source, but some can not, much as one might like to do so. There are church communities that draw the means to influence the masses from abstract and mysterious sources. Others again try very hard to be concrete. To these latter, parenthetically noted, belong the Mennonites. The Mennonites demonstrate what a tradition of hundreds of years can achieve in this respect. They turn with suspicion from everything that is mysterious and impenetrable. They base this on two fundamental principles: God is the source of all that is clear, good, and logical; the devil is the source of all that is dark and contradictory.

I suggested that it was especially desirable that a person's thinking, speaking and acting should not be governed by mass hypnosis but rather based as far as possible on clear understanding. But since such clear understanding does not seem to follow from objective research based on observation, we base ourselves on the word of the Lord: "The natural man cannot understand about the Kingdom of God," and so we preach that one

---

[1] Most Mennonites who settled in the Russian empire came from the North Sea city of Danzig (modern day Gdansk). Previously part of the Kingdom of Poland, Danzig became part of Prussia in the late eighteenth century when Poland was divided up by the great European powers. As a result, Mennonites found themselves again in a hostile setting, and welcomed the invitation by Tsarina Catherine II (1762-96) to settle in the Russian empire.

should be born again with the strongest emphasis on the person. At natural birth one is placed into the world as a person, separated from the mother, but not independent. But one is also captured by the mass hypnosis [of sin] in which there is nothing but the suffering of servitude and slavery. Only by the second birth through the Word and the Spirit of God is a person lifted out of the mass to become independent. The hypnotized mass will lose its value as a unity as soon as the hypnosis is dispelled. Once the hypnosis is gone the mass would necessarily crumble. That is why the enemies of the state see as their goal the destruction of the authorities in order to dissolve the masses in the most audacious meaning of that word. Their insidious labours would represent no danger if instead of a mass there were a humanity, composed of persons which would mature into a unity to the degree that in their personal search for truth they came to objective truth. It is that truth that Mennonites are after.

I drank from my glass while the forester drew on his pipe, which had gone out during my meditation. With some difficulty he got it going again. His eyes, it seemed to me, were blinking cheerfully, though whether from the smoke of the pipe or from deeper causes, I could not tell. Clouds of smoke again migrated towards the fireplace and the forester looked into the glow of the pipe with earnest thoughtfulness. "You're right," he said. "We should have such a humanity [75] but we don't. Its goal would be to strive without wavering for the objective and therefore the absolute truth. However, I have a question for you, a practical question about the present: do you believe that your church is such a unified body of the reborn?" "No, I do not believe that," I answered. "There are two orientations among us, one of which is very concerned to admit only those who are born again, and which also in part believes that it is successful in keeping away those not born again." "Right," he said. "And are these two orientations both represented in our detachment?" "Certainly." "Hmmmm." He shrugged his shoulders, and I looked at him and wondered what he was after. "It's just that – on that saint's day, you remember, when we had the bear hunt, ... I have to say that I made my observations then, and I noticed absolutely nothing of two orientations. There was remarkable unity. It appears to me that in your churches too there is still a kind of servitude; the functioning of mass suggestion can be detected. I really believe that we could exploit that for the benefit of the detachment and its work. Naturally I am against every abuse in such things, but a rational use of mass suggestion can surely do no harm. As long as we have no humanity we do well to lead the masses purposefully, even if it means leading them by the nose. I say this only in justification of the church to which I still formally belong." After a period of reflective thought he continued. "Yes, among us we make the leaders responsible for their movements among the people."

I had noticed that the lemon was missing on the tea table today. I was beginning to see that my dear, amiable superior had intended to make my tea tart by other means when he invited me.

Apparently he had at first thought that we Mennonites had matured more as human beings than the bush farmers of Liudinka. He had expected from us that we would do the good from personal initiative. The bear hunt had demonstrated to him that we, too, lived in a kind of mass hypnosis, that we had been led astray, and that we needed to be brought back. He never let on to what degree he held me responsible for the behaviour of the detachment. In any event, from that day on he began to manipulate the detachment with a very obvious, simple method. I was surprised at the relative ease with which we allowed ourselves to be manipulated and to react in the expected manner.

But the detachment manipulated the forester as well and even found a way of "dodging" away from this remote Liudinka. In [76] the end, however, the forester was better at it than we and held the control in his hands. His final words on that evening about the Catholic [Orthodox] church making its leaders responsible for the erring of the masses gave me pause. This much was clear, that from his point of view, the forester held me responsible for the goings-astray of the detachment.

There I stood, in the middle of a whirlwind of contradictory demands that were made on me. It was totally impossible to establish a legal basis for my attitude and actions. It is generally impossible. As boringly monotonous as life sometimes appears to be, one case will be totally unlike every other. Wherever laws are set up to deal with categories of cases, mistakes are common, for life consists of unique cases and not of categories of cases. Each case has to be decided on its own merits. That is why Jesus established the one and only law of love, but demonstrated in each case how he solved the questions and what it was that governed his decisions. Besides, Jesus has sharpened the human conscience. If a person allows himself to be led by the Spirit who manifests Himself in the conscience, all will be well. And whenever a case becomes quite impossible for us, our faith in His power to work miracles really sets in. We fly to Him, bring Him our impossible case, and He solves it for us.

Thank God, I did not stand in this whirlwind all alone, "the only sensitive heart among hypocrites." O no, there were quite a number of born again persons who knew something about the kingdom of God, who were striving to learn from Him "who is gentle and lowly in heart," and who allowed themselves to be led by the Spirit. We gathered around God's Word on weekday evenings for Bible study in addition to the Sunday worship. We experienced the blessings of the Saviour in the remote forest of Liudinka.

In this place amid such whirlwinds many an honest Mennonite fought his battles as Mennonites so often do, in silence and suffering. In the preceding reflections I have illuminated what, in my view, hurt our people. But all that does not imply that therefore we have no right to exist. Rather, in those deplorable shortcomings were concealed also the special tasks which were given to us. Christ "is set for the fall and rising of many" also among Mennonites so that "the thoughts of their hearts may be revealed." [Luke 2:34-35]. All those who despite forestry service and privileges, despite church and brotherhood, nevertheless came to a personal experience of God and did not become the victims of the circumstances, but mastered them – they are the fortunate.

* * * *

How interesting and pleasant it is to be surrounded by [77] people and to be able to love them. How many truly splendid people there are if one makes the effort to penetrate beyond the externals! I do not wish to relate a lot of details here. If it please God, I will someday tell you about them in separate stories and present them to you as Johannes Stein & Company. I will fictionalize the story so that they will never recognize themselves and you will not either. I will, however, make every effort to present them as they are, and to relate their life experiences as truthfully as it is given to me to do.

At this point only a couple of anecdotes which actually took place. In some cases, one does not know whether to laugh or to weep.

One morning when the detachment was at work, I was making the rounds of the barracks to look to several sick men and so happened to come into the dining hall. Before I got there I heard someone singing with a loud, clear voice:

> *O man, be wise, for time is fleeting*
> *And wisely use each hour you're giv'n.*
> *For only once you make this journey,*
> *Let all your footsteps point to heav'n.*[2]

The singer, who was bent over some activity, did not notice my presence. He was totally absorbed in his work. "How are things?" I asked. "Always happy?" "OK, middling to fair," he answered as he held out an old postage stamp in his hand, looking at it intently. "What are you doing?" I inquired. "Not much," came the reply. "I'm just cleaning some old stamps." "What for?" I continued. "Why, to use them again," he answered confidently. "Is that possible?" "Of course. On some the colours don't hold, but many are just fine. My wife only had to pay a fine once." I said: "Can you do this without protest from your conscience?" He looked at me with surprise. "Why not?" "You know that you are committing fraud, don't you?" I came back. "Fraud? What do you mean? Whom am I defrauding?" "Well," I said, "The government, the country, the whole nation!"

He could not comprehend my point. Was he not in all things a true Mennonite, baptized as an adult, regularly attending divine worship,

---

[2] This is a the first verse of a well-known hymn, popular with Mennonites: *"Die Zeit ist kurz, O Mensch sei weise, Und wuch're mit dem Augenblick. Nur einmal machst du diese Reise; Laß eine gute Spur zurück."*

clean-living, and a first-rate farmer? How then could this re-using of postage stamps be fraud? No indeed! It was just plain frugality. Country? Nation? These were alien, distant concepts to him. These were for him the realities which had always persecuted and oppressed Mennonites. This decent man had never compared his service to the service of those who were in the trenches, but [78] only with the circumstances of those who did not need to serve at all. And he could therefore not regard his service as either a privilege or a favour. He simply owed no one anything, and no one suffered when he sent letters with used stamps. As I went through the door and turned again to look at him, I noticed that his rigid and uncomprehending gaze had been following me. What was going on in his mind as he sat and looked at me? He knew that I was *gegrommt*. Our conversation had doubtless convinced him that other, much more serious errors lay hidden in me. This man came once to one of our Bible studies, but only once so far as I am aware. He did not understand the language we spoke there. Mass suggestion? Liberated personality?

How sad and dangerous it is, if a person is no more than Mennonite, Lutheran or Catholic! I don't know how things stand or stood with Lutherans or Catholics. Unfortunately, I know that there were Mennonites who sang "Let all your footsteps point to heav'n," and then travelled home absent without leave with forged documents. These were those for whom Mennonitism with its laws, privileges and advantages had become a snare.

But there were also others for whom that same tradition had become the soil for vigorous growth. A small, sickly man had the task of transporting sawdust from the basement of the sawmill out to the yard with a wheelbarrow. It was a task that was beyond his strength. I had succeeded in getting him a job that gave him a little more free time. I told him about it while he was emptying his wheelbarrow in the yard. He stood still, looked at me for a moment, and said: "Would it not be better if I stayed at this job?" "Why?" I asked. "I've got my work here," he replied, "and I can do it with a good conscience. I experience no temptations except that I get very tired sometimes. It may be different in the job you are offering me, and I don't know whether I could stand firm. You'd better leave me here." He was right to the degree that the position I wanted him to take was a position of trust. He would be thrown together with others who would test him as the *muzhiks* and the *desiatky* once had tested me. But the work was much cleaner and lighter than what he was now doing. "Think it over carefully before you turn me down," I said. "Such [79] an opportunity will not soon come your way again." He hesitated for a moment. Then he replied: "I thank you for your good will and for thinking of me. I knew that I was not alone. But please leave me here. Perhaps later sometime."

But enough of that. If I go on to tell of what happened next it would be discovered who he was and I want to avoid that. I merely want to show that there are people who are not just Catholics, Lutherans, or Mennonites, but who beyond that are conscientious and good and are activated by motives which are neither unreasonable nor reasonable; they rise above human reason and persuade the person to make reason captive to the obedience to Christ. One more thing I will say in defence of the Catholics, Lutherans, Mennonites and many other denominations: there are those, sometimes fewer sometimes more, who, very quietly, unobtrusively, and without drawing attention to themselves, pursue their small obligations and fight the good fight of faith. Yes, there are such people among the Mennonites as well, and although one barely sees or notices them, they are the light of the world and the salt of the earth.

Therefore, every case must be decided on its merits, conscientiously and faithfully.

* * * *

So there is psychotherapy which begins with the assumption that the patient must develop hope and confidence in the physician. Or should I adopt the method of Gerassim Pavlovich and insist on respect? I found the latter even more impossible than the former. But how was I to win the trust of patients when I did not understand the art of being a physician, and did not deserve to be trusted?

At 7 p.m. I had to go and meet my patients. Now I had to make the best of a bad bargain and act as though I knew something when in fact I knew nothing and could do nothing. The whole thing appeared to be desperately untruthful. Even though I may have known more about it than others, should I perhaps rather pile lumber and roll logs than play at being a physician? Did my office as preacher and the little bit of Latin I knew – but which could only be seen with a magnification of 1200 – did these justify my presence here? I was at the point of becoming deeply reflective.

Actually I was not a total novice in psychotherapy. In the good old days when we still had time for humbug, Dr. Otto Pinker had given me a detailed [80] lecture describing how one could become a doctor of miracles. First one had to create the odour of omniscience. One needed to learn to know only the symptoms of an illness, and then become familiar with the incubation period and the onset of the crisis by consulting an encyclopaedia. One of two things would happen; the sick would either recover or die after the crisis.

Supposing one suspected that a patient under one's care had pneumonia. The best course of action would be to say that one did not yet know what the illness was, but that a medicine would be given by which the illness would identify itself. One could give bread pills or coloured water and then wait. Should the crisis come and the man's nose turn unusually pointed and blue, then one should say: "Now I know what it is, but I am unable to help. The poor man will die." This sad prediction would then normally be fulfilled, and the weeping family would say: "He told us what would happen." This outcome would be a long step toward evoking trust.

But if the crisis arrived and the pointed blue nose did not show, then the opportunity would be there to adopt the most dignified bearing that could be found at a moment's notice, and say: "Now I know what it is. I will give you a medicine and it will surely help." And so one would give a bread pill or syrup water, depending upon what one had given before the crisis. Recovery would be virtually certain now, and the reputation of the physician established. Dr. Pinker mentioned various illnesses which were very good for this approach because they would be easy to identify and which in the crisis would mean either death or recovery.

So one could do that in an emergency, and would certainly avoid disaster for the patient. But the first condition, Dr. Pinker allowed, was not easy to satisfy, namely the correct diagnosing of the symptoms.

But my patients' trust in me had been established before I ever emerged from the labyrinth of my doubts back to the light of day. I heard someone stomping on the wooden sidewalk toward the clinic even though it was only three in the afternoon. As he neared I heard a loud and important panting, and when he emerged around the corner, he turned out to be our Gerassim Pavlovich. He ordered me to prepare splints, lignin, etc., since one of our boys had just broken his leg on the job. He, Gerassim Pavlovich would set it and put a cast on immediately.

In haste I gathered all that had been requested, [81] and was not yet finished when the injured man was brought on a sleigh and into the clinic. When, on orders of Gerassim Pavlovich, I removed his boots, he roared as though he had been skewered, and with good reason, for he had broken his leg in the lower third of his shin. The medic reassured me concerning the cries of pain from the patient, that they always did that and that it was by no means unusual. Then he judged that pulling off the boot had set the bone and now he would only have to put a cast on so that it would stay in place. He took a heavy splint, put some lignin on it and let it protrude an inch below the heel. Then he took two splints, laid them along the man's shin, took a wide roll of bandage and began to wrap it around the leg. The longer he wound, the more restless the patient became. He began to groan and finally he screamed as though beside himself. Undeterred, Gerassim Pavlovich kept winding the bandage, commenting casually to me, "They all do that." After he had finished he left, proud as a peacock. He would return at 7 p.m. to take a look at the cast.

Our patient screamed more and more despairingly and finally said he would rather I shoot him than leave him in this agony. The others who lay there supported him and begged that I remove the bandage. We were no longer satisfied that they "all did this." I had been present before when bones were set and had observed the application of splints and could testify that the procedure was not without pain. But when it was over, and even during the application of the cast, the patients always immediately felt better. They did not always behave like our patient, at least not in the medical practice at home. I could also see clearly why he had so much pain. The medic had wound the bandage too tightly around the splints, and had forced the bone apart again – if, indeed, removing the boot had ever brought it into the right position – and this might well cause pain. What was to be done?

Quickly I adopted the mask of omniscience according to Dr. Pinker's instructions, and said I was ready to put everything in order. But only if they all promised not to tell Gerassim Pavlovich. The promise was given immediately and joyfully, and I removed the bandage. Whether the bones had actually been set when I removed the boot I was no longer able to tell, but that they were no longer [82] set would have been obvious even to a blind man. Now came the part for which I had to take myself firmly in hand. Two of the other patients had to grip the leg at the foot and the knee and pull as though they were going to pull it apart. They did it clumsily, both of them shaking with fear, while the patient again in full measure did "what they always do." With my thumbs I tried to force the bone back into the proper position. I did it with about the same skill with which my assistants did the stretching. Suddenly I felt an odd jerk under my fingers, and my assistants, as though they had felt it too, relaxed their tension as if on command. The patient stopped yelling. The break had been set and now only needed to be secured. I padded the splints again, but I got so much lignin on the main support that it did not touch the heel. However, my assistant repaired it so that it fitted the contour of the leg. The new bandage was applied and everything was fine. I was a bit concerned that Gerassim Pavlovich would notice it and become angry. However, he came, saw the bandage, praised it and pointed out to me certain advantages of doing it that way which only he, in his extensive practice had learned to apply, and that the other medics in the area knew nothing about.

When he asked me why I looked so pleased I could answer him quite honestly that it was because I was so happy over the success of the cast and that the patient now felt so well. "Yes," he said, "He is lucky. Sometimes they yell for three days before the pain subsides." "No wonder," I thought, but did not say it.

Although my assistants had promised to be silent, the news did get around the detachment that I had changed the bandage. My reputation as a bone specialist was firmly established. Our famous bone specialist in the Molotschna also prepared a special medicine, and achieved many successful cures. Thus, by association, it was assumed without my having to lie about it, that I too could do all those things.

I was an unqualified success as a physician. I am able to boast that 100% of my patients survived, and, with the exception of the epileptics, were cured. I constantly marvel at it. It still happens that acquaintances ask me to examine them. If I always laugh when I take the stethoscope in hand, it is because it helps to set them at ease.

Gerassim Pavlovich taught me to deal with the "scabs" [83] in a playful way. It was his view that every illness produced a fever condition, and that the "*febris lodderis*" (the Russian word *loddyr* means "lazy-bones") was no exception. It was only that the fever condition in this case was more concealed, and therefore, in order to determine the temperature, the thermometer had to be rubbed gently. Quinine was the best medicine against "*febris lodderis.*" It had to be administered in a solution, and he gave me the recipe for it which included a little addition of hydrochloric acid. The "scab" received a little whiskey glass full of this devil's brew before bedtime. If not successful, he should return again in the morning for another dose. This potion kept the "scabs" away from then on. But there were a few incorrigibles. They came again and again, until finally I sent them away. I told them honestly that I did not believe them, and they were not even offended by it.

* * * *

In addition to my work in the emergency room, the drugstore, and the sick bay, I was also responsible for keeping the records of the assets and liabilities of our institution, and not only to administer the medicines, but also replenish our stock, which was very difficult. There were no strict rules and regulations for acquiring what was absolutely necessary. And when there were rules, they were interpreted differently at each time and place so that one never knew how to begin. One was successful only if one could "smell" correctly.

Orel was the nearest town at which we should have been able to buy our medical supplies, but they were not available there. Just as impossible was the attempt to purchase in Moscow. Only in Kharkov at the "Iurotat" was it possible to achieve anything. And that is where I had to go. Never will I forget those journeys in crowded cars and with totally unreliable passenger train schedules. When I went on these trips, the forester gave me a certificate which stated that I was the padre of the detachment. This opened the door for me to be somewhat more confident with the officers, to travel second class, and if necessary, to speak a firm word to the station commandant. It is by no means certain that, had I been a soldier, I would by now have even the first delivery of supplies in Liudinka.

Before my departure, Gerassim Pavlovich and I had prepared a list of medications which we needed, regardless of whether we were allowed to have them in our drugstore or not. We were not allowed to stock volatile chemicals since we had no qualified dispenser nor a qualified doctor in our institution. But we had to have them [84]. Where would we be able to get hydrochloric acid which was so important to the treatment of *"febris loddcris?"* Once the list was complete, the forester would brood for a while about how the forbidden medications could be acquired. Then he would give me the list with the instruction that I was to get all of them, even if they had to be stolen. I never resorted to stealing, but mostly I got what I went for. I also often got medications like aspirin, guaiacol and others when they were already scarce in Russia and not available anywhere else.

When I returned with my loot the records had to be "fixed."[3] I brought them to the forester "unfixed", just as I had them in my note book. All the bribes and the *tolkachi* were noted in detail. *Tolkachi* means "pusher." If there was an incline in the track over which the locomotive alone could not pull the train, a *tolkach* that is, a second locomotive, was brought in, which pushed from behind until the train was over the mountain.

---

[3] Janzen's concern with bribes and special favours is understandable considering the time he lived in. More than four years of war, internal strife, civil war, and several revolutions had destroyed Russia's financial integrity. Inflation spiraled out of control, as Bolsheviks even wondered briefly if a cash economy was even necessary given the anticipated world communist revolution. As a result, questions of integrity were daily raised, and demanded a response.

But let me begin at the beginning. I go to pay for my train ticket. Any ordinary mortal would simply be refused, but I show my documents. I travel as a clergyman under orders from a crown enterprise. They cannot refuse me a ticket. But the cashier regrets deeply that every seat has been taken days before so that he cannot give me a ticket today. As a Russian official I now become indignant, imperiously demand my ticket, and push the money through the wicket. The cashier quickly calculates how much is there and notes that it is five rubles more than the price of the ticket. He yields to the coercion. "Gentlemen," he says loudly, "I take no responsibility. I am forced to give him a ticket. I have no protection against these military types (*woennoe*)." "*Ne razgovarivai!*" (Stop blathering!) I growl at him as I take my ticket, and the *muzhiks* who stand around deferentially make way for me. They believe that my authority had secured the ticket for me. "*Vot tak Popp!*" (He is some priest!) they say knowingly to each other.

I, of course, know that it was not my authority but the extra five rubles that got me the ticket. Everyone except the *muzhiks* knows that. And everyone regards it as totally normal. My forester knows it too, and the whole administration, every office, right up to the ministry. Everyone is pleased when someone under orders finds ways and means, [85] despite the laws which regulate the traffic, to get from one place to another. The five ruble bribe has done it for me.

In Kharkov I turn my list in at the office of the wholesaler. The director returns with the list personally. With a thick red line he has crossed out all the medications we may not legally have. I protest, but nothing can be done. The director cannot give me these volatile medications and that is that. I look very disappointed and proceed to get what can be got. In the dark passageway to the forwarding department I slip ten rubles between the pages of the order. The clerk takes it and checks it through. "I believe you will give me everything I have ordered," I say to him casually. "Impossible!" he says. "How can I give you what the director has crossed out?" He pages through the order, and suddenly his face lights up. "Well," he says, "Let's see. *My eto delo obtjapaiem*" (We'll fix it somehow). It takes days until everything is packed, but finally all is ready for transport.

I travel with it to the train station. "What have you got there?" says the baggage clerk. "Medications," I reply. "Oh, for the transport of medications you need permission from the district commandant," he says. I don't even know whether there is a district commandant. I doubt it. Again the wheels will not turn because they lack grease. If I now begin to look for the district commandant they will send me from Herod to Pilate. Meanwhile my supplies will likely be stolen from the baggage room, and the attendant will complain because I have left the crates there. He does not wish to keep an eye on them and besides, there could be flammable chemicals in there . . . .

Well and good; ten more rubles find their way unobtrusively into the pocket of the baggage clerk, and suddenly everything runs as if greased. I stay there until the crates are transferred. Then I finally refresh myself after the day's labours with a simple meal, and after a while I embark, that is, I force myself into the narrow passage of a second class carriage and stand there jammed in until the next transfer point where I need to change trains and where my provisions also have to be transferred. I go into the baggage room immediately and am told firmly that my wares cannot proceed on this train since all the baggage cars are already overfilled. [86] Now the affair is much too heavy for the usual locomotive; a *"tolkach"* has to be brought up. Another five rubles find their way into the pocket of the baggage attendant and the matter is done. There is enough room and I have only to make sure that I keep up with my crates. At first I can only find standing room on the carriage step. Gradually, with the leaving and entering of passengers at the various stations, I make my way step by step into the interior of the car and finally even get a seat. When I finally arrive at our camp, I proceed with my receipts to the forester in order to "fix" them all there. *"Nu chto, protolkalii?"* (Well, how did it go? Did you manage to get our supplies past all the obstacles?) *"Tak tochno, portolkal."* (At your service, I did it). Then we proceed into his private office and "fix" the papers. I have receipts for two thirds of the actual amount spent. The forester finds that very satisfactory, judging by his own experience. The other third has to be covered, and we do it. And the bills pass every office without hindrance. Everyone knows how it is done because that is the way it has to be done.

All that gave me some bad hours, and I could only justify it on the grounds that I did not take a single kopek of it for myself. How good I feel here in Canada where, over these four years, I managed to get everything that I needed without paying even one cent of a bribe. Certainly there are dangers here too, but one is not hopelessly condemned to untruthfulness. One can easily fall into sin here in Canada as well, but one is not compelled to it by brute force. Here we still have time to gather supplies for the time when they will be needed. Let us not neglect these days of grace.

* * * *

In February, 1917, a silence fell over Liudinka that was quite eery and lasted for three days. No mail arrived. No telegrams were delivered or sent. Trains left irregularly and did not return. After three days we learned that the emperor had abdicated, and that the reins of government were now in the hands of the imperial duma.

Happiness returned. [87] No longer did we need to worry about our loved ones. For with the passing of the tsarist regime, all its orders would also become invalid. Indeed, we hoped that there would now be peace. An interim government was constituted, but from the beginning there was an evil shadow – the soviets in the Tavrida Palace – which, like Peter Schlehmil's shadow, soon grew over the head of its begetter, despite the fact that it was and remained only a shadow.[4]

During this time I changed from a physician into a politician and diplomat, and in that capacity I learned that the doors of officialdom were

---

[4] The events that unfolded in 1917 were exceedingly complex, and resist easy explanation. The Tsar's abdication in February 1917 left the Russian empire without a logical political successor. As a result, the Parliament (Duma), whose term had expired, declared itself to be the national government on an interim, or "provisional" basis, until national elections could be held. At the same time, workers and soldiers sought their own governance in councils *(Soviets)* that were established in the capital and elsewhere. Initially both political bodies met in separate wings of the Tavrida palace in Petrograd (St. Petersburg today). Janzen's reference here to the Soviet as the "evil shadow" makes it clear which political body he supported.

open much more readily to the commoners than before. It was done, however, only to welcome the visitor with fine words and to get rid of him again with clever words, and to do it in such a way that the visitor did not know whether anything had been achieved or not.

We had no lofty goals in mind for our diplomacy. We wanted only to be given the same rights as all the others who served. In diplomatic fashion we did not mention our obligations in the memorandum submitted to the Provisional Government. We also requested and received leave from service. Finally, we urged that the law of liquidation be revoked, but in that we failed. On this issue we were admitted to the office of Kerensky's legal aid, Mr. Morduchai-Boltovski.[5]

During our third visit to his office a smile crossed his face in an unguarded moment which told me more than all the words that followed. This was the way it was. The law was clearly unjust, but it could not be abrogated at this time. We had to be fobbed off, any way that was possible. After that smile I was no longer concerned with words. I would have preferred to break off diplomatic relations then and there and declare war. But as a Mennonite I could not do that and so I had no alternative but to abandon my diplomatic career.

Little by little our detachment was dissolved. As a teacher, I was released from service by order of the Kerensky government and went back home to my family.

Then came the "red" period during which decent people had to be satisfied simply to exist if they could and were allowed to do so. To act had become totally impossible. The night had come, during which no man can work.

---

[5] Alexander Kerensky was a moderate socialist and a lawyer by training, who attempted in 1917 to bridge the gap between the Provisional Government and the Soviet. However his ambitions clearly exceeded his abilities. Kerensky became the Prime Minister of the Provisional Government in July, and was blamed for all of its failures when it disintegrated in the early fall of 1917. Kerensky fled St. Petersburg in October of 1917 as Bolshevik forces under Lenin's direction were preparing their final assault.

In Liudinka I had been forced to act unlawfully. Everyone knew it was unlawful, but also that it was unavoidable. Now what was unlawful and unjust was made into law. If, as loyal citizens we wanted to participate publicly, we [88] had to be re-educated to regard public robbery and theft as lawful and proper. The war, whose thunder we had heard from afar, now came into our midst and invaded the very depths of what we were. It was no longer the war of nations which, after all, was governed by certain laws. Here it was civil war, fratricide in its worst expression. The events of that time wrenched our lives and tossed us about. We were unable to influence it in any way. Our hands were tied.

Our conscience rose up in strength against what the time now demanded of us. It was no longer a matter of cleaning off a few postage stamps. The question was not whether what the circumstances demanded of us was right or wrong. The issue was no longer whether we could or should pay bribes to get something that was needed. Here it was a matter of living and dying. The struggle was quite openly in favour of the material against all spiritual realities. Contradicting the words of Jesus, the principle was nailed down: "Man lives by bread alone." Now we either denied our faith or we suffered and died for it. The privileges were gone without a trace. They turned into their opposite and became for us the cause of virulent enmities and persecutions.

It took a while before we were clear about where we stood. But we did achieve a clarity that enabled us to take a stand. Blessed were those who took that stand toward the light and toward justice, and who still do. Even today they are pilgrims from the cross to the crown, beyond the thorns to the stars. Woe to those who took a stand for darkness, and who still do. They wander on arid desert paths to perdition despite all the drivel about culture and progress. God's winds were blowing and separating the wheat from the chaff. They have not yet stopped blowing and will do their work thoroughly. We Mennonites had a long period of rest in Russia during which, separated from other peoples, we could develop. And there was much there that was good which others did not have. Then came the war and the time of testing; the protective walls fell and we were required to prove what value our spiritual riches were to the world. We failed at many points. Our excellent institutions could survive only as long as we remained together in solidarity and in separation.

But the fire that burned in some hearts spread, and the time of testing taught us as never before that the value of a society can be measured by the number of capable and dedicated people it can furnish to the world in times of need.

Then came the time of persecution which taught us that [89] those who desired to live a godly life in this world will certainly be persecuted. It taught us that a great gulf was fixed between light and darkness which cannot be bridged by any compromise. Here there is only a death and life struggle. Now it occurred to us whether perhaps we would have been better off if, from the beginning, we had taken persecution upon us rather than accepting all sorts of compromises such as bribes and the like. Over against the world our people came to the conclusion: No to the world, and cling to Christ! The question for the individual is whether the lessons our people learned with great struggle in times of distress will be accepted and used.

I feel as one who has sat beside the road and observed people passing by, their struggles and wrestling, their victory or their defeat. It is as though God himself had directed me to the road of life and to those souls who walk on it until they disappear into perdition, or finally find the strait gate and the narrow road of life and strive to enter the Kingdom of God and be saved.

It is this that constantly urges me to lift the veil, to look at the causes, to remember what I have seen and share it with others. It is to constantly urge them [toward the good], although they rarely understand me and I usually get blows on the neck instead of remuneration.

I look for persons in the masses, and as soon as I find them, I will show them to you.

15 January, 1929.

Acknowledgements

The pen and ink drawings reproduced in this book are the work of Johannes Janzen, elder brother of Jacob H. Janzen. They were used originally as chapter heading illustrations in Jacob H. Janzen's book *Den Meine Augen haben Deinen Heiland gesehen* (Hamburg: Christliches Verlagshaus Wiegand, n.d.).

The family photographs on the following pages, as well as the cover photo of Jacob H. Janzen, come from the collection of Hardy and Erika Janzen, whose kind help and cooperation is hereby recognized.

We acknowledge with thanks the permission granted by CMBC Publications that allowed us to use the photographs of the Mennonite Church at Gnadenfeld, the High School for girls at Tiege, the Old Berdjansk Forestry, and the Red Cross train on the cover background. The photos were reproduced from Gerhard Lohrenz, *Heritage Remembered. Revised and Enlarged Edition. A pictorial survey of Mennonites in Prussia and Russia* (Winnipeg: CMBC Publications, 1977).

A final and special thanks goes out to Philip Neufeld, whose dedicated efforts contributed much to bringing this book to the light of day.

Illustrations

Jacob H. Janzen and Helene Braun at the time of their marriage in 1899.

Top: *The Mennonite Church at Gnadenfeld, Molotschna, where Jacob H. Janzen was ordained pastor in 1906.*
Bottom: *Jacob H. Janzen at home in his study, sometime between 1908-1915.*

Top: *The high school for girls in Ohrloff – Tiege, where Jacob H. Janzen taught from 1908 - 1915.*
Middle: *The Old Berdjansk Forestry, where Jacob H. Janzen served in 1915.*
Bottom: *The Jacob H. Janzen family around 1917. Back row (L to R): Jacob, in Russian Army chaplain's uniform, holding Marta; Erna. Front row (L to R): Helga, Heinz, Eliesabet, Helene, Sieghard, Alexandra.*

Jacob H. Janzen around the time of his emigration to Canada in 1924.

About Pandora Press

Pandora Press is a small, independently owned press dedicated to making available modestly priced books that deal with Anabaptist, Mennonite, and Believers Church topics, both historical and theological. We welcome comments from our readers.

Leonard Gross, *The Golden Years of the Hutterites*, rev. ed.
    (Kitchener: Pandora Press, 1998; co-pub. with Herald Press).
    Softcover, 280pp., index. ISBN 0-9683462-3-5
    $22.00 U.S./$25.00 Canadian. Postage: $4.00 U.S./$5.00 Can.
[Classic study of early Hutterite movement, now available again]

The Believers Church: A Voluntary Church, ed. by William H. Brackney
    (Kitchener: Pandora Press, 1998; co-pub. with Herald Press).
    Softcover, viii, 237pp., index. ISBN 0-9683462-0-0
    $25.00 U.S./$27.50 Canadian. Postage: $4.00 U.S./$5.00 Can.
[Papers read at the 12th Believers Church Conference, Hamilton, Ont.]

An Annotated Hutterite Bibliography, compiled by Maria H. Krisztinkovich,
    ed. by Peter C. Erb (Kitchener, Ont.: Pandora Press, 1998). (Ca. 2,700
    entries) 312pp., cerlox bound, electronic, or both.
    ISBN (paper) 0-9698762-8-9/(disk) 0-9698762-9-7
    $15.00 each, U.S. and Canadian. Postage: $6.00 U.S. and Can.
[The most extensive bibliography on Hutterite literature available]

Jacobus ten Doornkaat Koolman, *Dirk Philips. Friend and Colleague of
    Menno Simons*, trans. W. E. Keeney, ed. C. A. Snyder
    (Kitchener: Pandora Press, 1998; co-pub. with Herald Press).
    Softcover, xviii, 236pp., index. ISBN: 0-9698762-3-8
    $23.50 U.S./$28.50 Canadian. Postage: $4.00 U.S./$5.00 Can.
[The definitive biography of Dirk Philips, now available in English]

Sarah Dyck, ed./tr., *The Silence Echoes: Memoirs of Trauma & Tears*
    (Kitchener: Pandora Press, 1997; co-published with Herald Press).
    Softcover, xii, 236pp., 2 maps. ISBN: 0-9698762-7-0
    $17.50 U.S./$19.50 Canadian. Postage: $4.00 U.S./$5.00 Can.
[First person accounts of life in the Soviet Union, trans. from German]

Wes Harrison, *Andreas Ehrenpreis and Hutterite Faith and Practice*
    (Kitchener: Pandora Press, 1997; co-published with Herald Press).
    Softcover, xxiv, 274pp., 2 maps, index. ISBN 0-9698762-6-2
    $26.50 U.S./$32.00 Canadian. Postage: $4.00 U.S./$5.00 Can.
[First biography of this important seventeenth century Hutterite leader]

C. Arnold Snyder, *Anabaptist History and Theology: Revised Student Edition* (Kitchener: Pandora Press, 1997; co-pub. Herald Press). Softcover, xiv, 466pp., 7 maps, 28 illustrations, index, bibliography. ISBN 0-9698762-5-4
$35.00 U.S./$38.00 Canadian. Postage: $5.00 U.S./$6.00 Can.
[Abridged, rewritten edition for undergraduates and the non-specialist]

Nancey Murphy, *Reconciling Theology and Science: A Radical Reformation Perspective* (Kitchener: Pandora Press, 1997; co-pub. Herald Press). Softcover, x, 103pp., index. ISBN 0-9698762-4-6
$14.50 U.S./$17.50 Canadian. Postage: $3.50 U.S./$4.00 Can.
[Exploration of the supposed conflict between Christianity and Science]

C. Arnold Snyder and Linda A. Huebert Hecht, eds, *Profiles of Anabaptist Women: Sixteenth Century Reforming Pioneers* (Waterloo, Ont.: Wilfrid Laurier University Press, 1996). Softcover, xxii, 442pp. ISBN: 0-88920-277-X
$28.95 U.S. or Canadian. Postage: $5.00 U.S./$6.00 Can.
[Biographical sketches of more than 50 Anabaptist women; a first]

The Limits of Perfection: A Conversation with J. Lawrence Burkholder 2ⁿᵈ ed., with a new epilogue by J. Lawrence Burkholder. Rodney Sawatsky and Scott Holland, eds. (Kitchener: Pandora Press, 1996). Softcover, x, 154pp. ISBN 0-9698762-2-X
$10.00 U.S./$13.00 Canadian. Postage: $2.00 U.S./$3.00 Can.
[J.L. Burkholder on his life experiences; eight Mennonites respond]

C. Arnold Snyder, *Anabaptist History and Theology: An Introduction* (Pandora Press, 1995; co-pub. Herald Press). ISBN 0-9698762-0-3 Softcover, x, 434pp., 6 maps, 29 illustrations, index, bibliography.
$35.00 U.S./$38.00 Canadian. Postage: $5.00 U.S./$6.00 Can.
[Comprehensive survey; unabridged version, fully documented]

C. Arnold Snyder, *The Life and Thought of Michael Sattler* (Scottdale: Herald Press, 1984). Hardcover, viii, 260pp. ISBN 0-8361-1264-4
$10.00 U.S./$12.00 Canadian. Postage: $4.00 U.S./$5.00 Can.
[First full-length biography of this Anabaptist leader and martyr]

Pandora Press, 51 Pandora Avenue N.
Kitchener, Ontario, Canada N2H 3C1
Tel./Fax: (519) 578-2381
E-mail: panpress@golden.net
Web site: www.golden.net/~panpress

Herald Press, 616 Walnut Avenue
Scottdale, PA, U.S.A. 15683
Orders: (800) 245-7894
E-mail: hp%mph@mcimail.com
Web site: www.mph.lm.com